S0-BYE-375

IF I'M SO SUCCESSFUL, WHY DO I FEEL LIKE A FAKE?

THE IMPOSTOR PHENOMENON

JOAN C. HARVEY, Ph.D.,
with CYNTHIA KATZ

PUBLISHED BY POCKET BOOKS NEW YORK

Grateful acknowledgment is made to Random House, Inc., for permission to quote from *Bright Lights, Big City*, © 1984 by Jay McInerney.

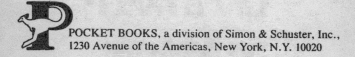

POCKET BOOKS, a division of Simon & Schuster, Inc., 1230 Avenue of the Americas, New York, N.Y. 10020

Published by arrangement with St. Martin's Press
Library of Congress Catalog Card Number: 85-50867

ISBN: 0-671-61749-4

First Pocket Books printing January, 1986

10 9 8 7 6 5 4 3 2 1

POCKET and colophon are registered trademarks of Simon & Schuster, Inc.

Printed in the U.S.A.

To my sons,
Stephen and Daniel

Contents

Author's Note

The personal stories and comments that appear in this book have been gathered throughout the past few years in my work on the Impostor Phenomenon. They come from several sources: discussion with patients I have treated and participants in studies I have done; conversations with people suffering from the Impostor Phenomenon; and interviews conducted specifically for this book with men and women in different parts of the country.

To protect the identities of the individuals involved, all the names have been changed and biographical details have been altered or disguised. In some cases, stories and/or comments have been combined to form composites.

Acknowledgments

First and foremost, I want to express my warmest appreciation to Cynthia Katz for the professional skills, perceptiveness, sensitivity, and sense of accuracy that she devoted to this book. Working with her was a real pleasure.

I am deeply grateful to the many people who have shared their personal experiences and private "impostor" feelings with me. Their generosity and openness have contributed a great deal both to this book and to my own understanding of the Impostor Phenomenon.

I would also like to thank my professional colleagues who have so graciously shared their thoughts and research findings with me. In particular, I'd like to express my appreciation to those who have been involved in studying this syndrome. Our discussions and debates about the Impostor Phenomenon have always been enjoyable and enlightening.

To my agent, Julia Coopersmith, goes my gratitude for all her help and support.

Finally, I'd like to say a very special thank you to my editor, Victoria Skurnick. This book—and I—have benefited greatly from her wise advice, skill, enthusiasm, and dedication.

The Terrible Secret

ONE

It's a feeling of fear. I always have the sense that I'm not going to get the job done, and that I'm not necessarily qualified to do it. That I'm never going to pull it off or give them whatever it is they want. And it creates a sense of panic in me that they're going to find out I'm doing a terrible job and should be fired—and that I'll never work again.

—Leslie, graphic designer

Impostor. Fake. Fraud.

These are words that conjure up very definite images. Images of people who pretend to be something they are not. People who set out to deceive us in some way, who have come by good fortune through dishonest means.

Such people do, of course, exist. There is the con artist who swindles others with his phony stories. The forger who cashes bad checks. Every so often we read about someone practicing medicine with false credentials. All these people fit the bill as impostors, fakes, and frauds.

But there is another kind of person who believes these same words apply to him. He* knows he hasn't lied to others or misrepresented his credentials. He knows he has worked hard for his success. Yet, he feels, "I am nothing but an impostor and a fake. I don't deserve my success; I haven't really earned it. I've been fooling other people into thinking I'm a lot smarter and more talented than I really am."

He doesn't tell anyone his terrible secret, but waits in anxious dread to be discovered. He is certain that the moment of discovery will arrive, and he will face

_____
*To avoid awkward sentence construction, I use the pronoun "he" to mean both "he" and "she." No sexual bias is intended.

unbearable humiliation and be stripped of his undeserved success forever. At that moment, he will be exposed to the world as a fraud.

On some level, this person is well aware that he has studied and trained for his career. He realizes he has accumulated an impressive list of accomplishments over the years. Other people have seen his work, and regard him as bright and competent. None of this changes his conviction that he has earned his success under false pretenses.

Why would such a person think of himself as a fake, a fraud?

He is a victim of the Impostor Phenomenon.

WHAT IS THE IMPOSTOR PHENOMENON?

The Impostor Phenomenon is a psychological syndrome or pattern. It is based on intense, secret feelings of fraudulence in the face of success and achievement. If you suffer from the Impostor Phenomenon, you believe that you don't deserve your success; you're a phony who has somehow "gotten away with it." You aren't the person you appear to be to the rest of the world.

But there is far more to the Impostor Phenomenon than that. The sense of being a fraud is only one part of it. Victims of the Impostor Phenomenon are caught up in a cycle of emotions, thoughts, and actions that can virtually control their lives. Although they are often people who are driven to achieve, they live in fear that each new success will reveal them as fakes. They are sure that when this happens, everything they have labored so hard to build will be destroyed.

Despite the evidence, to a victim of the Impostor Phenomenon, none of his success seems real, none of it earned. Yes, the corporation president can see that he is doing well: He brings new business into the company, earnings are up since he took over the job, the board and the stockholders are pleased with the results he's achieved. But if he suffers from "impostor" feelings, he looks at his own success and concludes that he faked his way into it.

Other people may make the "mistake" of thinking this person is bright, creative, and gifted. He remains secretly convinced that he is mediocre, unqualified, incompetent, even stupid. And, for some people who suffer from this syndrome, the more successful they get, the more severe and crippling it becomes.

The Impostor Phenomenon is not limited to the world of work. Many people feel that they are frauds in some area of their personal lives as well. In this chapter, we'll look at how you can feel like an impostor at work. Later on, you will see how this syndrome affects people in other areas of their lives.

WHO IS A VICTIM OF THE IMPOSTOR PHENOMENON?

It is now believed that as many as *70 percent* of all successful people have experienced feelings of being impostors or fakes at some point in relation to their work. We can't even guess how many people must have lived with these kinds of feelings in past generations. Yet it is only recently that we have come to recognize and understand the Impostor Phenomenon.

Victims of the Impostor Phenomenon are people who lead perfectly normal lives. They marry, have children, function—and often excel—in their work. They carry their "impostor" feelings inside. But they are "regular" people. You, me, the couple down the block.

The Impostor Phenomenon is not selective about

choosing its victims. Men and women, the young and the old, and members of any race suffer from the feeling of being a fraud. And the Impostor Phenomenon affects people in every type of occupation. Executives, performers, doctors, teachers—all can feel convinced they are impostors, their achievements a "mistake."

The Impostor Phenomenon goes hand in hand with the idea of success. But that doesn't only mean the top-of-the-ladder, rich-and-famous kind of success. You don't have to be a world-famous movie star, corporation president, or Nobel Prize–winner to suffer from the feeling of being a fake.

It is true that if you feel like an impostor, you must have accomplished *something about which* to feel fraudulent. You must have attained *some* measure of success. However, success can be defined in whatever terms are relevant to your own life, in any area in which other people have recognized you as successful.

The young management trainee who receives a promotion has achieved one kind of success. The artist who has his first gallery show has achieved another. The real estate agent who makes his first sale has achieved still a third. All these people are experiencing success in what they have attempted to accomplish. It is not imagined or simply longed for; they have concrete evidence of success.

Assuming you have accomplished some type of success, your particular *level* of success doesn't determine whether you will or will not suffer from the feeling of being a fake. You don't have to achieve a dramatically high level of success. The Impostor Phenomenon is related to *how you feel about a particular role you are playing*. The people in the examples above are playing the roles of young executive, up-and-coming artist, and new real estate agent. They are successful in *these roles*. Even at this level of success, they are susceptible to the Impostor Phenomenon if they don't believe they are qualified to play their roles, don't deserve to play them, or, for whatever reason, simply don't belong in them.

In 1980, I designed the Harvey IP Scale, a list of statements that measures how strong the Impostor Phenomenon is in an individual.[1] I gave this scale to a group of 72 college juniors and seniors. Half these students were in honors programs; the other half were taking more typical college courses required for their majors.

These were simply students. Not top-ranking executives, rock stars, or famous novelists. But, *as students,* some of them had achieved more public success than others by virtue of participating in an honors program. And, as a group, those very honors students scored *significantly higher* on the IP Scale than the other students did.

Their success was limited to achievement in school; impressive in one sense, but not the same as "making it" in the working world. Yet even that level of success was enough to bring out strong feelings of phoniness and self-doubt.

This doesn't mean that the other students—the ones not in the honors programs—were free from "impostor" feelings. Many were undergoing the same experience. For most of them, however, it was less severe. The higher scores of the honors students show how the Impostor Phenomenon can grow worse as one receives more public recognition for success.

Although the Impostor Phenomenon is not a new problem, it wasn't until 1978 that the syndrome even had a name. The term "Impostor Phenomenon" was coined by two psychologists at Georgia State University, Dr. Pauline Clance and Dr. Suzanne Imes. They had been observing this phenomenon for several years, studying 150 highly successful female students and career women.[2] Despite good grades, honors, awards, advanced degrees, or promotions, these women persisted in believing that they were less qualified than their peers. They suffered from a terrible fear of being "found out" as impostors.

Word spread about this "new" phenomenon, and other psychologists began to study the syndrome. In 1980, psychologist Jeanne Stahl and three colleagues talked about a study they conducted with a group of black female college students.[3] The results were astonishing: *93 percent* of these women showed signs of the Impostor Phenomenon in attributing their academic accomplishments to something other than intellectual characteristics.

Researchers were finding the Impostor Phenomenon among all sorts of people. In 1984, Dr. Margaret Gibbs, Karen Alter-Reid, and Sharon DeVries reported on their study of the Impostor Phenomenon.[4] They had sent out questionnaires to licensed psychotherapists, whose names were simply selected from a national register of doctors. These therapists were asked to respond anonymously about their own feelings. Had they ever had the sense of being a fraud or impostor in their work?

This was a random sample of qualified professionals. Surely, you would not expect to find feelings of fraudulence in such a group—particularly among therapists, trained to understand emotions.

Out of the 84 responses, *69 percent* reported that at some point in their work as therapists they had experienced the feeling of being an impostor.

The same year, psychologist Dr. Gail Matthews of Dominican College reported another study she had conducted with Dr. Clance.[5] This study involved 41 men and women in a variety of occupations. Among them were an entertainer, a judge, an attorney, and a scientist. Of the people in this group, *70 percent* said they had experienced the Impostor Phenomenon.

In truth, we are only beginning to understand how widespread the Impostor Phenomenon may be.

By their very nature, some careers tend to promote the Impostor Phenomenon (IP) in someone who is susceptible to it. Certain kinds of work demand that we constantly take on different and new tasks. This is frequently the case in creative pursuits. The writer, movie director, architect, or fashion designer continually moves from one project to the next. If you have "impostor" feelings and work in such a field, you may fear that each new project is the crucial test that will finally reveal your lack of creative talent.

If an IP victim can't come to terms with his feelings, the Impostor Phenomenon may become a constant problem, plaguing him throughout his career. No amount of success or recognition eases the psychological pain, or releases him from the fear of being exposed as a fake.

When these feelings are severe enough, they may actually prevent someone from having any success at all. Dr. Mary Topping raised this question in 1983 after doing a study of the Impostor Phenomenon involving 285 faculty members at two large Southern universities.[6] Along with several other psychological tests, she gave the Harvey IP Scale to 157 women and 128 men. Topping found that the lowest-ranked professors (presumably, those who were new or hadn't been promoted) had stronger IP feelings than the more established, higher-ranking faculty members.

"Is it possible," she wrote, "that those who suffer from the IP remain at the lower faculty ranks or exit (voluntarily or not) from the institution?"

We have not yet learned how many people are

"casualties" of the Impostor Phenomenon. Some IP victims may never accomplish what they are capable of because their fears continue to hold them back. Some may flee from their career paths altogether if the IP is too strong for them to combat.

It is difficult to know how many people have achieved less than they should have, or have given up completely, due to the Impostor Phenomenon. We can't easily identify those who "might have been" successful if they hadn't believed they were fakes. The professors in Topping's study who didn't suffer from feelings of fraudulence had either resolved the issue somewhere along the way, or never felt like impostors in the first place. If the IP had caused any faculty members to give up their career goals altogether and drop out of the competition, they wouldn't have been around to participate in the study. Undoubtedly, there were a number who had already switched to other careers, ones that didn't bring on these troubling feelings.

THE THREE SIGNS OF THE IP

The three basic signs of the Impostor Phenomenon are all present in anyone who is an IP victim. They are as follows:

1. The sense of having fooled other people into over-estimating your ability.
2. The attribution of your success to some factor other than intelligence or ability in your role.
3. The fear of being exposed as a fraud.

Let's consider these three signs, one by one.
We know that the person with "impostor" feelings has indeed achieved some measure of success, what-

ever it may be. The people around him view his accomplishments as objective evidence that he is qualified and capable. But he sees things differently. Within himself, he lives with the feeling that he isn't what he seems to be. A discrepancy develops between the way he sees himself and the way in which others see him.

This discrepancy is the first sign of the Impostor Phenomenon. The person is sharply aware of the difference between his public image and his private one. He feels like a phony who has fooled other people.

Even as his successes accumulate, a victim of the Impostor Phenomenon can't accept them as evidence of his own talents and abilities. He doesn't "internalize" success—take credit for it and use it to nurture a sense of mastery and pride. His secret belief that he isn't smart enough or talented enough surrounds him like a wall. Success can't penetrate this wall to change his thinking.

So how does this person explain all the evidence that contradicts his feelings of phoniness? A new job title, a salary increase, new assignments, honors, awards, praise from experts—these are all proof of his abilities. If he is as incompetent or unintelligent as he believes himself to be, how did he get where he is today?

This is where sign number two enters the picture.

The person who feels like an impostor does have an explanation for his success. He will attribute it to almost any cause *other* than genuine ability. He may say that he works harder than anybody else in his office and has succeeded only because of his Herculean efforts. Or, he might believe he is "getting by" on his charm, social skills, flair, glibness, or good looks. He will suggest it's all been a matter of good luck, pure and simple. Or, perhaps those who evaluated him made an error in judgment. Some of the people I interviewed truly believe their promotions were due to clerical errors!

Victims of the Impostor Phenomenon offer all types of explanations for their achievements. "I only got this job because I had the right connections." "They gave me the contract because I was in the right place at the right time." "Standards are low in general." "Luck was with me. I can't assume it will happen again." "I got the promotion because the boss finds me attractive." "They needed a token woman."

Anything *except:* "Because I'm smart and talented, and I deserved it."

Ryan is a successful advertising copywriter. When I asked him how he had gotten where he is today, he thought for a minute and said: "I think I've gotten where I am through circumstances. Most of the jobs have been through connections or somebody recommending me. Jobs came to me. I'm not exactly sure why, but I've been lucky. I think perhaps I didn't deserve those jobs because I didn't really try to get them. They just sort of appeared.

"And I think my personality has a lot to do with it. People have a tendency to like me. I'm easy to get along with. I don't generally create problems for anyone. I think people like that."

In 1980, Jeanne Stahl and her colleagues conducted another early study of the Impostor Phenomenon.[7] This research included 41 young black women from 12 high schools in the Atlanta area. All were science majors, between the ages of sixteen and eighteen, in their senior year at school with high aspirations for their future. The group's mean grade point average of B indicated that they were high achievers.

As the psychologists reported, *over half* these women attributed their achievements primarily to something *other* than intelligence. Instead, they saw their success as the result of hard work, perseverance, or determination. Almost one third of them felt that their achievements were due to *luck* 50 to 75 percent of the time.

The reasons IP victims offer for their success can be quite broad ("I'm good with people") or specific to a particular situation ("I got the job because the company president is an old family friend"). Some say they just don't know why they've been successful, but they're still convinced that it wasn't due to their own abilities.

Factors such as business contacts, personal charm, and simply being in the right place at the right time certainly can help us achieve our goals. But the key word here is *help*. These things are only one part of what it takes to succeed. They will take us just so far if we don't have the ability to do the job. The person who feels like an impostor doesn't see this. He believes that these other factors are completely, or at least primarily, responsible for his accomplishments.

Many who suffer from the Impostor Phenomenon are extremely intelligent and talented. They often possess a variety of personal assets: efficiency, self-discipline, the ability to put other people at ease—the list goes on and on. However, even if they are aware of having certain abilities, they minimize them. In fact, they don't view them as skills at all. In their eyes, the things that come naturally and easily to them are expected, taken for granted. They don't "count."

What counts varies from person to person.[8] But for the IP victim, it is always *that one area in which he sees himself as being weak*. It doesn't matter how much evidence he has that he is skilled in other things. To him, the things he is good at just aren't very important.

One manager knew she had good telephone skills, but felt she was weak in her writing abilities. She thought she was simply "getting by" by using the telephone a lot; being able to write a good report would be the true measure of communication skills. For the person who is better at putting together letters and memos, it may well be the telephone skills that are seen as the true measure of competence.

A victim of the Impostor Phenomenon is certain that other people are wrong about him. He believes he isn't a bright, capable person; he's just been successful because of some natural gift or some bit of luck. It is impossible for him to have any lasting enjoyment of his success. He is too caught up in dreading what will happen when others find out he has fooled them. We have come to sign number three: the fear of exposure.

If you have experienced the fear of being exposed as a fraud, you know how painful it is. It is likely to create anxiety that seriously interferes with your daily life. You might recognize some of the signs of this anxiety in yourself: shakiness, sleeplessness, perspiring palms, shortness of breath, "butterflies" or cramps in the stomach, decreased appetite or compulsive eating, diarrhea, and tension headaches.

In 1983, Dr. Mary Topping specifically researched the Impostor Phenomenon in connection to anxiety.[9] The successful person who feels like a fake already knows what she scientifically proved. The two are strongly related. Anxiety goes along with the feeling of being an impostor.

An IP victim usually feels his anxiety intensify when he anticipates that—as one IP victim described it to me—"the big one" is coming. "The big one" is any event that someone believes has the potential to expose him as a fraud. For the businessperson, it can be a crucial report or client presentation; for the Ph.D. student, it is often the dissertation oral exam; for an actor or movie director, it may be the next film on which he will work.

One man, a computer programmer for a large corporation, imagined that "the big one" would take the form of a complex computer program. He pictured this program as containing all the computer tasks he had never done before. Each time he was to receive a new assignment, he would anxiously watch his boss's desk to see if "the big one" was there waiting for him.

The idea of being exposed as a fake, or as less than what one appears to be, brings on frightening visions. IP victims can't imagine how they would recover from the blow. Here are the ways three people described what would happen if others "found out" that they were impostors:

"It would mean losing all that I've done to date. It would erode the bedrock my career is built on. For them to say 'he has no talent' about me would be so dreadful. I'd go find a rock to hide under; I wouldn't want to see daylight."

"People would ostracize me and eliminate me from the society of respectable, productive people. I would have to return to my little, safe home where I guess I feel I can manage okay."

"A sense of loss, floating, not knowing what to do. I depend on past experience to get work. If I were found out to be 'not good,' what would I do? I'd kill myself."

Because they dread being exposed as fakes, IP victims often share another fear. This is the fear of failing. To them, any failure is going to be the give-away, the event that shows the world they are only impostors. But some are not just *afraid* of failing; they are terrified of it. And they tend to define failure as *any mistake or flaw that reveals them to be less than perfect*. Anything short of brilliance or perfection brings out the IP victim's self-doubts. So any event that he sees as significant—or, as I call it, any "performance event"—holds the potential to bring his imaginary house of cards tumbling down around him.

To the person who feels like a fraud, the idea of failure means total disaster. These are the words IP victims use to predict the consequences of their anticipated failure: "They'll fire me." "I'll flunk out of school." "Everyone will laugh at me." "I'll be humiliated in public." "I'll never work again." "They'll think I'm a nothing." "They won't ever speak to me again." "I'll end up on welfare." "They'll kill me." "No one will ever love me." "If I fail, I might as well be dead."

One executive expressed a feeling shared by many IP victims: "Failure is an unacceptable condition. I'll do anything to prevent it. In thinking of failure, the shame and embarrassment is untenable. I just couldn't bear it."

The IP victim knows that he fears failure. Strangely enough, on another level, he may also fear success. Later on, we'll look at the reasons why someone might be afraid of success, and how the fear of success relates to the feeling of being a fake.

The Impostor Phenomenon involves more than just ideas and feelings. It also affects the way a person *acts*. People who believe they are frauds adopt certain ways of behaving to hide this "fact." They may, for example, become "workaholics," trying to stave off the exposure they dread through backbreaking effort. Many people realize they are acting in a driven way, but have no idea why they are doing it.

In Chapter 2, you will meet all the different types of "impostors," and see how their behavior patterns may relate to you.

When you add up the IP victim's thoughts, feelings, and actions, the Impostor Phenomenon syndrome is complete.

Neil is a talent agent working in a large West Coast company. Forty-three years old, he is intelligent, friendly, and outgoing. Before coming to this agency three years ago, he had spent six years with another firm in his field, and entertained a number of job offers before deciding to join up with his current employer. His career has progressed steadily, and he is doing well in his job. He has been singled out several times for special attention and praise from the head of the agency.

None of Neil's accomplishments have changed his belief that he is an impostor. "I'm very clever and fast, and I *look like* I know what I'm doing," he explained. "But really, I don't know anything, and one of these days people are going to find that out with a bang."

He concedes that he is bright, and describes himself as "fairly creative when I allow it." But Neil feels that it is his personality that is "almost totally responsible" for his professional success. Even as a child, he was known in his family for his warmth and gregarious personality. As he sees it: "Who I am is pretty much 'Let's make sure that everybody's happy all the time.' I'm so funny and charming that I make people feel good, glad to be around me."

"Very few people are as charming as I am as often as I am, especially in groups. I'm a presence in a place, and it has very much worked to my advantage. In meetings, people listen to me. They think I'm smart." With this type of personality, he says that "people tend to think you're tremendously on top of things. They don't know that *you* don't know what the hell you're doing."

When Neil is complimented for his work on a project, he describes his reaction as one of fear: "I'm immediately afraid that it's the last time I'll pull off something like that. I think, 'Yes, what I've done is great—and it'll be the last great thing I'll ever do.' I'm beset by doubts. When people assess my projects, I always believe the person who thinks the least of what I'm doing. If twenty people think something I've done is terrific and one person has even a hint of doubt, that one is the one I'll listen to."

In Neil's eyes, all of his charm and abilities in getting along with people are only a smokescreen. "I have sort of a false self," he stated. "It protects me from exposing just how boring and stupid I really am on the inside." Underneath his outgoing personality, he says, he is actually a private, quiet person who keeps himself emotionally isolated in many ways.

"The ways in which I'm an impostor are very convenient," reflected Neil. "There's a payoff—they work. That's why it's so hard to get rid of them. But the *feelings* aren't at all convenient. I can't stand the idea of feeling this bad for another fifteen years. I just can't see being sixty-five and still feeling like I'm fooling people all the time."

THE UNRECOGNIZED SIGNALS

Despite the fact that the Impostor Phenomenon is a very real problem for many people, it often goes unrecognized and untreated, even when it is quite debilitating. One reason for this is the secret nature of the IP. When someone believes he is a fraud, he doesn't want other people to know about this "fact." If word got out that he is an impostor, he fears, that would be the end of his job, his friends, and, possibly, other people's love for him. So IP victims usually don't discuss their feelings—not even with their spouses or closest friends. They go to great lengths to hide their terrible secret.

A second reason is that psychologists may not immediately recognize signs of the Impostor Phenomenon in someone who comes to them for help. For one thing, our understanding of this problem as a distinct psychological syndrome is still very new. And, as several of us have observed in treating patients with the IP, people entering psychotherapy who feel like frauds seldom mention this as their chief complaint. It is only later on that the feelings painfully emerge.

The person with "impostor" feelings who comes for therapy usually talks about a variety of other problems. Some of the more common ones are procrastination, insomnia, feelings of dread when waking up in the morning, pounding of the heart, or tension in the jaw, neck, or shoulders. These can all be symptoms of the Impostor Phenomenon.

Some symptoms may be even more extreme. They can include drug or alcohol abuse, obsessive-compulsive thoughts and habits, and eating disorders such as bulimia (when a person repeatedly feels compelled to overeat and then vomit).

Of course, these symptoms can also be experienced by people who suffer from something other than the Impostor Phenomenon. But, over time, feelings of fraudulence and the dread of exposure can lead to such signs of stress. An IP victim may not understand exactly what the problem is, but he can tell that something is wrong.

If someone suffers from feelings of fraudulence and a fear of being exposed, then why do I say he may not understand what the problem is? IP victims typically don't see their belief that they are fakes as something that can be changed or treated. They don't think to themselves: "I *feel like* a fake." They think: "I *am* a fake." In their minds, they have been fooling the world into thinking they are something they are not. They believe that they truly are impostors. To *be* an impostor is part of their self-image, a core element of their identity. If I *am* an impostor, what can anyone say or do that is going to change that fact?

IP victims need to understand that they are *not* impostors. The truth is that they only *feel like* they are. And these feelings can be understood and changed.

NEW ROLES AND THE TEMPORARY "IMPOSTOR"

Not everyone who suffers from the Impostor Phenomenon experiences it in exactly the same way. There are different levels of intensity. Some people struggle with extreme feelings of fraudulence throughout their lives. They have severe cases of the IP, causing them great anguish and anxiety. Others have more moderate cases, certainly troubling to them, but able to be kept under control. Then there are those who have only mild feelings of phoniness.

No matter how strong or how mild your feelings may be, you should remember that certain situations increase your vulnerability to these feelings. For example, you are likely to find that your feelings grow more intense when you enter a new situation.

In new situations, you frequently must assume new roles. If you graduate from business school and are hired by a corporation, your role changes from that of student to businessperson. That means new tasks, new requirements, and a new self-image. But this is a role you have never played before. How can you be certain what is expected of you?

The person who finds himself in such a position may interpret his lack of knowledge about the role to mean that he isn't qualified to perform it. He might even begin to believe he has misled his employer about his abilities. But he goes on to perform the role anyway—all the while convinced he is a "fraud."

It takes time for new and unfamiliar roles to be incorporated into our self-image. During that time, an

IP victim tends to think his discomfort with the role is a sign that he is really an impostor, incapable of doing the job well. He doesn't see that his feelings are caused by the mere newness and unfamiliarity of the circumstance.

New situations that demand a certain level of performance from us can be quite anxiety-provoking. Under these circumstances, the idea that someone might feel like a fraud or phony is not surprising. There is a pressure to act as if you know exactly what you are doing in order to perform the functions and meet the expectations of the role. High achievers set high standards for themselves, so they feel the additional pressure of their own expectations. Inside, they may still wonder if they can "deliver the goods."

Unfortunately, IP victims tend to assume they should know immediately how to play a role to perfection. But everyone must endure some frustration until they learn a new role and come to "wear" it comfortably.

Matthews and Clance have suggested other situations that might bring on feelings of phoniness. When they did their study of 41 men and women, they found that "impostor" feelings were often associated with unexpected or unanticipated success. Some examples: early promotion, or being the youngest person ever to be elected to a particular position.[10]

Perhaps you recall having "impostor" feelings at one particular point in your life. For some people, the IP is only a temporary experience, cropping up for a period of time and then disappearing for good. It might come along with a new job, sudden advancement, a financial windfall, fame and recognition, or a public award or honor.

No matter what brings on the sense of fraudulence, the person who has only a temporary case of the IP experiences the same feelings as the chronic IP sufferer. He has the same sense of being unqualified and unable to meet the demands of the particular situation. He thinks he has fooled others into believing he is capable of handling the job. Anxiety and dread set in. He is afraid others will discover his failings and reveal him as a phony to the rest of the world.

Consider the person who is hired for a new job, or suddenly gets a promotion. In his mind, there is likely to be a great deal riding on the situation: his income, his reputation, his career plans—maybe just his desire to prove he can handle it. The work is new to him or more complex than in his previous position.

"I don't know how to do this job," he thinks. "Look at all these other people in my department—*they* know what they're doing. I'm not as qualified or as bright as they are. I don't know as much about this industry as they do. I'm just winging it."

"Impostor" feelings have sprung up in full bloom. He wonders how long it will take until he makes some catastrophic error. He questions why he got hired or promoted in the first place. And, like other IP victims, he comes up with an answer that has nothing to do with his abilities: "They must have made some kind of mistake. I knew all the right tactics to impress them in the job interview." Or, "The boss likes me because we both play tennis."

Many people are eventually able to overcome their "impostor" feelings. As they master their new roles, they are able to view their accomplishments as evidence that they are "the genuine article." The sense of fraudulence passes with time and with further proof of their abilities. They are able to break the cycle of success and self-doubt.

The new executive may come to accept his role. His suggestions have been used by the company with good results. He is getting positive feedback from his boss. Perhaps he even realizes that his co-workers have some of their own self-doubts and fears about their job performances. He doesn't expect that his work will always be perfect, but he learns that he can handle the job.

I believe temporary IP experiences are far more common than we now know. How many people are *so* certain of their abilities and intelligence that they don't ever wonder if perhaps they have "put one over" on others? Such a thought may only occur to us in passing—or it may take hold and flare up into the feeling of being a fake.

The fact that these feelings of fraudulence are short-lived in some cases doesn't make them any less painful for the person experiencing them. If you have experienced temporary feelings of being a fraud, you know how troubling they can be. They still rob you of the pleasure and satisfaction in meeting a challenge. But if you can recognize early signs of the IP in yourself, you can do something about the problem.

Leslie, aged thirty-four, is a free-lance graphic designer. She is hired by companies on a project-by-project basis to design the look and layout for everything from brochures and annual reports to publicity handouts and book covers. Prior to going out on her own, she spent four years in the art department of a publishing company. After six years as a free-lancer, she has established an excellent reputation in her field and is completely self-supporting.

Leslie feels she is a phony on two fronts. Both her parents are painters and highly intellectual. Having grown up in an atmosphere in which fine art was revered, she doesn't think that the type of work she does qualifies as "real" art; it doesn't meet her parents' standards. She also doubts her own creativity; she wonders whether her work meets even the standards of its own world.

"I may not want to do this, but it's part of how the

world sees and judges me," she said. "No matter what I did, I'd want to excel. I feel I'm not excelling, I'm not the best, not innovative. So I feel like I'm not qualified and I shouldn't do it."

This feeling "comes up more often now being a freelance person because I work on new jobs all the time with different people," Leslie explained. "Also, I'll apply, and always have, for jobs that I have no track record for. It's this funny combination of knowing that I have no certifiable credentials to support my claim that I can do something, and at the same time, I'm willing to try and go do it. But once you find yourself in the middle of the situation where people say, 'Yes, go do it,' then you go, 'Oh, my God, what have I done? I'm just hot air.'

"All my past positive experience doesn't reinforce me. It's like I'm not learning. The fear remains just as intense. But it also depends on the job—how many people I have to show my work to, who it is. The fear increases with the number of people involved."

In the full-time positions she's held in the past, Leslie experienced the same doubts about her abilities. "I was convinced they thought I was qualified for the job, but that I wasn't at all," she said. "Which would make me work really, really hard in the beginning. Generally, after a couple of months, I realized I was capable of doing the job, and then I would sort of relax a bit. That doesn't necessarily mean I felt I was *good* at it, but that I knew I could get by and do it, and no one would say anything. The fear would come up again when new projects would arise."

Part of her success today is due, in Leslie's eyes, to a "maniacal obsession with hard work." She was "a serious workaholic for a good four or five years. I sort of burned out; I can't really do it as much. I probably haven't stopped being a workaholic, but I *feel* like I stopped." Leslie sees the slow periods when jobs are scarce as "penance" for not keeping up the same rate of hard work. "I feel like you get punished if you don't work that hard," she reflected. "Yet I can't quite summon it up to do that anymore, and I feel like in some intangible way there's a relationship."

Along with her hard work, Leslie believes she has been helped by good luck and her ability to get along with people and to charm them. Although it has taken many years, she has found that hiding her own feelings and constantly accommodating others is a high price to pay for their approval. Now, she says, "Occasionally, I'll have a bad meeting with people in a business situation and it stuns me. I don't expect those things to go wrong. I know how to listen. I know how to anticipate. I know how to sort of read what I think somebody's looking for. I had *years* when I never got a negative reaction. So I'm stunned when I get them. And I get them much more often than I used to. I find that very confusing."

AN AMERICAN SUCCESS STORY

We should consider the American attitude toward success and achievement. Our culture places a great premium on success and many people are driven in the extreme to attain it. Some have grown up believing that failure is shameful, that anything short of absolute success with a capital "S" is unacceptable.

Americans are also taught early on that success is available to anyone who wants it and is willing to work for it. Though many people have argued over whether there is truly equal opportunity for all, the idea has been a constant theme throughout this country's history. We talk about "upward mobility." In fact, there are countless examples of people who have reached heights their parents never dreamed of.

Then there is the American work ethic—as a people, Americans are *supposed* to be hard workers. The message is reinforced: Other people have done it; why can't you? Get out there, don't complain, and make it happen. And, if you're bright, your success should be that much greater.

These notions can create very mixed feelings in us about how successful we should be, how success should feel, and what we can expect from it.

Daryl, a playwright in his mid-thirties, has doubts about his image as a truly creative artist. He wonders if he deserves the recognition he gets for his work, and if he can keep coming up with creative ideas. He talks about what success now means to certain "baby boomers" like himself who come from families of privilege.

As Daryl points out, in general, each generation surpasses the previous one in terms of material and educational attainments. "I look at it in terms of the 'cake' and the 'icing,' " he said. "The 'cake' for one generation was just having a house and a car. The 'icing' was greater educational and professional attainment. For the kids of that generation, going to college was the 'cake'; getting a graduate degree or a really hot job was the 'icing.' I think that was pretty much my parents' generation.

"In my view, for us, it all became 'cake.' Many of our parents went to law school or medical school, or were businesspeople with high positions. Now the 'icing' is excelling in these things. Becoming a doctor is no big deal. Becoming the chief of surgery at a major hospital—*that's* a big deal. For my friends, a show on Broadway is success. For a while. Then you have to have another one. Success becomes defined in terms of this constantly moving thing."

If we believe the idea that success is available to us, we may be motivated, or feel obligated, to go after it. And with the pursuit of success may come self-doubts. Questions arise in our minds: Am I as qualified or competent as the people around me? Do I deserve success?

If we go on to achieve some of that success, it can bring with it a lot of anxiety and confusion about who we "really are." Am I the same poor kid who used to play stickball on the street? Or am I this important executive who crisscrosses the country in a company jet? Which of these self-images is the "real" one?

Confusion about our identity can be even worse if we find ourselves catapulted to success quickly. We hear a great deal about the "overnight success" story. A classic example is the unknown actor who opens in a Broadway show and suddenly is the toast of the town when the theater reviews come out in the morning. Yesterday he was a struggling actor; today he is a star. In the course of twenty-four hours, his public image has changed. How does this affect his image of himself? Few people find success as quickly as this, but many of us have seen our lives changed by success in a relatively short period of time.

All of this provides fertile ground for the Impostor Phenomenon to take root.

WHAT THE IMPOSTOR PHENOMENON IS NOT

People sometimes ask me if the Impostor Phenomenon is really the same thing as insecurity or low self-esteem. Isn't feeling like a fake just a part of being insecure about oneself? Or, aren't these problems just the same as having a low opinion of oneself?

There *is* some relationship between the Impostor

27

Phenomenon and insecurity. But insecurity is a very broad concept. It can involve a wide range of feelings and behaviors. Insecurity does include feelings of self-doubt and a lack of self-confidence, and an IP victim experiences these feelings as well. However, insecurity is not a specific syndrome, with specific, identifiable symptoms. I have never found any test to measure insecurity in an individual.

The Impostor Phenomenon, on the other hand, is a *distinct type* of insecurity. It is not just a matter of "being insecure." The IP is a syndrome that can be clearly defined and identified. It is a series of specific feelings, with particular ways of behaving and thought patterns. And, unlike general insecurity, it is typically associated with a drive to achieve at some level. We can measure the intensity of the IP in an individual. There are specific courses of action designed to help someone overcome it.

You can feel insecure without having the sense of being an impostor. For example, one type of insecurity is the fear of "losing it all," imagining that everything you have will disappear tomorrow, and you'll be left poor and alone. The basis of this fear might be in a past trauma, such as abandonment by a parent, sudden poverty, war, or persecution. Some of those who suffer from the IP share this fear, but, in their cases, it is based on the idea that they will be exposed as frauds.

Another difference between general insecurity and the IP is the ways in which people deal with them. If you feel insecure, you can handle that feeling in many ways. You may or may not show it in your behavior. You may discuss your insecurity with your friends and not worry about keeping it a secret. It doesn't necessarily carry the same shameful connotations or fears of personal exposure as being an "impostor."

If you believe you are an impostor, you have probably kept it a secret. Most IP victims never consciously betray their feelings of fraudulence in anything they say or do. It's likely that you don't really believe there is much you can do to alter this secret aspect of yourself.

Because some people say they feel they don't deserve their success, they might assume the Impostor Phenomenon is nothing more than guilt. Later on, you'll see how the IP sometimes involves guilt. But guilt is not always present in the person who feels like a fraud. It is only one aspect of "impostor" feelings.

What about low self-esteem? It frequently comes as a surprise to people to learn that the Impostor Phenomenon and low self-esteem are not the same thing, nor are they related in any significant way. Some people suffering from the IP may actually have very high self-esteem.

Self-esteem has traditionally been defined and measured by psychologists as a kind of all-or-nothing situation. In other words, you either have esteem for yourself in all areas, or you don't have it in any areas at all. It is usually considered a very general feeling of positive self-regard—not something that can be added up, part by part.

This is not the case for victims of the Impostor Phenomenon. They often have a highly positive regard for many of the qualities they possess. They feel like impostors in *one particular area*—but may feel perfectly fine about themselves in areas outside this one. They believe they are lacking only in some quality significantly related to their role: creativity, intelligence, management skills, or whatever talent is relevant to what they do.

The person with low self-esteem in its true sense is typically *not* a high achiever. IP victims commonly have a drive to achieve, so the person whose self-esteem is very low is missing something essential to the definition of an IP victim. In extreme cases of genuinely low self-esteem, a person might become a criminal, prostitute, or drug addict. IP victims are definitely not in that category. Their self-esteem is usually high enough to allow them to reach high places. Those with low self-esteem often remain among the lowest ranks.

Unfortunately, that one quality the IP victim believes he is missing is also the one that he believes is the mark of true ability, the quality that "really counts." He points to some other personal asset he knows he possesses—social skills or good looks—and assumes it is the real explanation for his success. Even though he takes his other skill or asset for granted, he places *too much* value on this quality when he uses it to explain his success. For example, Neil, the talent agent, knows he has a warm personality and has very positive feelings about himself in this regard. However, he has overvalued this asset when he claims that his personality is the *only* reason he was hired for the job.

It's as if the IP victim stands before a balancing scale. On the left side of this scale is the particular quality that he believes would make him a "genuine" success (intelligence, creativity, etc.). On the right side are all his other personality assets. He tips the scale by placing all his self-esteem with his personality assets on the right side. What he needs to do is distribute that self-esteem so the scale will balance.

Sometimes, IP victims do reveal feelings of high self-esteem, even if they're not aware of it. An outstanding teacher with top qualifications called herself "marvelously mediocre." At one point, she went on interviews for three very different, desirable, and highly paid positions in her field. She was offered all three jobs. Her comment to me was: "I dazzle them with footwork and baffle them with bullshit." When I asked her how she was able to impress people so well, she admitted: "I can carry it off because I really know my stuff."

In describing his feeling of being a phony, a novelist explained: "I have no doubts about my skill—my craft, my trade. I'm a skillful technician. The doubts come in when it comes to creative ideas. Trying to be brilliant, wanting desperately to be brilliant, and ending up sometimes hackneyed and trite."

Said a marriage counselor: "I sometimes feel, 'Who am I to pontificate about anybody's life?' Not that I really tell people what to do, but clients expect us to give them advice. So sometimes you act as if you know, when you don't really. It's expected of you in your role. I know this is more a feeling than a reality. At one level, I know I'm really qualified to do what I do."

When I first began studying the Impostor Phenomenon, several of my colleagues raised this same question: Was the IP really low self-esteem? At the time I studied those 36 honors students, I decided to examine this more closely.

I measured the concepts, or constructs, of the IP and self-esteem in two ways. When students filled out the Harvey IP Scale, I also gave them the Rosenberg Scale, a list of statements with which they could agree or disagree. This scale is used to measure self-esteem. (As in my other studies, they didn't know what these scales were designed to measure, so they couldn't try to figure out what answers would be "best.") Then, they answered some open-ended questions. These were straightforward interview questions; rather than having to check off multiple-choice answers which I might provide, they could answer in their own words.

The results showed that the Impostor Phenomenon

and low self-esteem are definitely not the same thing. Very few students who had strong IP feelings also had low self-esteem. And very few students who had low self-esteem also experienced strong "impostor" feelings. In terms of statistics, only 9 percent of the differences in one could be explained by the differences in the other; 91 percent couldn't be explained or accounted for. What this means is that *some* people with the IP have low self-esteem, but most do not. And some people with low self-esteem suffer from the IP, but most do not. The two concepts are separate and distinct from each other.

MY DAYS AS AN "IMPOSTOR"

I have written this book as a psychologist who has studied the Impostor Phenomenon and treated others suffering from it. But I know about the IP from another perspective as well, since I was also one of its victims.

I was one of the fortunate ones. In my case, the Impostor Phenomenon was temporary, and I was able to overcome it. But I know all too well the emotional pain of the IP victim. Let me tell you my story.

Like many IP victims, I had always been a high achiever. I started bringing home good marks in grade school and kept it up all the way through college. When I received a B.A. in journalism, I became the first one in my family to earn a college degree.

Shortly before finishing college, I got married. Next came children. At this point, my intellectual pursuits took a back seat to the raising of my family. I was still doing some part-time writing at home, secluding myself in an upstairs room for a few hours a day. But I treated this work more like a hobby than a profession. Most of my time was spent with my children, my days revolving around playgrounds, naps, and "Sesame Street." I still read—novels, mostly—but I was far removed from the academic life.

When my youngest child reached the age of four, I decided to go back to work. We had just moved to a new city, and I wanted to meet people and get involved in some different activities. So I began doing volunteer work in a psychiatric hospital. The philosophy in this particular hospital was that of a "therapeutic community." Everyone on the staff got hands-on training and became involved in the therapy process.

I then went to work at a general crisis telephone "hotline." I had the night shift, 10:00 P.M. to 9:00 A.M. Late at night, people called in with every kind of problem from paranoia to depression to suicidal feelings. I began to learn more and more about working with people to solve their problems.

After these jobs, I knew I wanted to become a psychologist. I applied and was accepted to the Ph.D. graduate program in psychology at Temple University.

When I arrived at Temple, I had no formal academic training in psychology. I didn't know the academic vocabulary of psychology or the procedures for research. I hadn't even been inside a classroom in years. Even though I'd had a lot of practical experience in my work, I felt that I knew far less than everybody else. They had studied psychology in undergraduate school and were familiar with all the jargon and statistics. And I was afraid the other students were just plain smarter than I was. I thought that if I were going to survive in graduate school, I would have to act as if I knew just as much as the others. I began to feel I was a fake.

This feeling became almost overwhelming in one seminar I was taking. Anyone could sign up for these seminars, so as a newcomer, I was thrown in with third- and fourth-year students. The other students were so articulate. They seemed so knowledgeable. I didn't understand half of what they were saying (because, of course, I hadn't gotten as far in my studies as they had). Yet I sat there pretending to comprehend absolutely everything.

At the end of the term, we were all required to give a presentation before the rest of the class. I was terrified. I felt my speech had to be perfect, and that *I* had to be perfect when I stood up to give it. I managed to get my presentation scheduled as the last one of the semester. But I began working on it before any of the other students had started theirs.

To prepare for the big day, I wrote down everything I planned to say on index cards and then memorized it all. I repeated my speech into a tape recorder, attempting to make it sound natural and casual. Then I drew up a handout for the other students delineating the points I planned to make.

I didn't want to have a single vulnerable point that might lead to my exposure as a fraud. I purposely made the presentation overly long so there wouldn't be much time for questions afterwards. Why give the others a chance to expose any flaws in my argument or in my knowledge of the subject? Even so, I was prepared with a strategy for handling questions: I would get the students to argue with one another, instead of with me. Just throw the question at someone else: "Oh, didn't *you* say something about this point?" That way, I would have a discussion going without having to participate in it. I also picked out the most striking outfit I could find to wear. I thought, "If I'm no good, at least they can enjoy looking at me!" In my mind, this assignment had become "the big one," the one that would reveal me as a fake.

On the morning of the big day, I left for class two

hours early (just in case the car should break down, or some other unforeseen horror should occur). I took my index cards so that in the event of total amnesia I could read aloud word-for-word. I felt like throwing up.

After beginning my presentation, I realized I wouldn't need the cards. I knew my topic well—much too well. I began to spontaneously change some of the phrases I had so carefully memorized and rehearsed.

Then, about halfway through, I saw a hand go up. One of the students wanted to ask a *question*—a question that held the dreaded possibility of revealing my ignorance and exposing me as a fraudulent graduate student. I went on speaking, attempting to ignore the hand, hoping it would give up and go away. But it was persistent and obtrusive. Soon everyone in the room had seen it. There was no way out. I had to let the person attached to the hand ask his question. It turned out to be the simplest and most obvious question I could have imagined. I answered it easily. Other students raised their hands and all their questions seemed elementary to me. I realized how overprepared I had been. No one even thought about—or cared about—the many intricate details I'd studied so meticulously. Even the professor's questions seemed basic.

My time "on stage" was over too quickly. My presentation received an A plus. But I was left with a very anticlimactic feeling. My adrenaline level had risen but had no place to go. My brain was storing trivial information for which I had no use. I felt as if I had prepared for a severe hurricane but only had to cope with a mild drizzle.

As you can see, all three signs of the IP were there. I believed I was a fake, fooling others into thinking I was smarter than I really was. I attributed my achievements to hard work, instead of to intelligence. And I was afraid my exposure as a phony was just around the corner.

Happily, my feeling of being an impostor subsided by the following year. I had learned the vocabulary of psychology and now understood what the more advanced students were talking about. I even came to realize that some of them didn't always know what they were talking about, despite their impressive words. I stopped feeling that others were smarter than I, or that I had to hide what I didn't know. I was able to accept my role as Ph.D. student and break free of the Impostor Phenomenon.

Although my own experience with the Impostor Phenomenon was only temporary, I still recall it clearly. It caused me great anxiety, and sapped me of my time and energy. It destroyed any enjoyment I might have gotten from those early days at school.

In this chapter, I have described only the broad outline of the Impostor Phenomenon experience. There is still a great deal more to be said. In the following chapters, we'll look at the ways that IP victims act in order to hide their "terrible secret," and more about what they think and feel in both their work and personal lives. You'll be able to examine if and how the Impostor Phenomenon is affecting you and what the causes of it might be. And, lastly, you'll see how to free yourself of the feeling that you are a fraud.

We have yet to learn how many people share the belief that they are impostors. Wherever I go, I find myself being asked about the Impostor Phenomenon. When I explain how an IP victim feels, some people immediately gasp, "But that's me!" Others are shocked to recognize themselves in the description of an IP victim. But they all want to know what it means, why it happens, and what can be done about it.

This book will attempt to answer all these questions. I hope that it will also help those suffering from the Impostor Phenomenon to understand the problem and realize they are not alone. Then they can begin to break the bonds of the IP, and go on to enjoy the successes they have earned and richly deserve.

Hiding the Secret

TWO

The feeling of being a fake is only one part of the Impostor Phenomenon. The IP also affects how we think and act.

People who want to hide their "terrible secret" of being an impostor tend to develop certain patterns of behavior. In this chapter, you'll see what these patterns are, and why it's so difficult for the IP victim to break free of them.

Some of these patterns were first identified early on in IP research, notably in the work of Dr. Clance and Dr. Imes. Others are additions I have made based on my own study and observations. For purposes of description, I have broken them down into different "types." As you read about them, you may recognize other signs of the Impostor Phenomenon in yourself, or in someone close to you.

Don't be surprised if you see yourself in more than one type. These patterns aren't mutually exclusive. IP victims may follow more than one at a time. However, as Clance and Imes observed, people seldom employ *all* of them. Usually, they favor one particular pattern or a combination of several.[1] And, how closely you match one of these IP "types" will depend upon how strong your "impostor" feelings are.

It's important to remember that these patterns have

two dimensions. They involve both behavior and thought. Simply engaging in the behavior alone won't necessarily perpetuate a feeling of fraudulence. Part of these habits is what we call a cognitive, or thinking, component. In other words, tied in with what the person does are his thoughts about why he is doing it.

These patterns then influence a third dimension: a person's feelings and emotions about himself. Unfortunately, the habits only serve to make the feelings of fraudulence stronger and more resistant to change.

IP TYPES

THE WORKAHOLIC

The term "workaholic" is a familiar one to most people. We've heard about the individual who is driven to work so hard he appears virtually addicted to it, much as an alcoholic is to liquor. Not all workaholics suffer from the Impostor Phenomenon. But workaholism is one of the IP syndrome's behavior patterns.

For an IP Workaholic, the long hours and intensive effort he puts into his work are only one part of the equation. This person not only works very hard, he explains his achievements as the result of hard work *alone*, or as *mostly* the result of hard work.

IP Workaholics begin to prepare for "performance events" far in advance of their peers. The department head starts working on his report earlier than the other managers; the student begins studying for an exam a month before his classmates do; the speechwriter fears that he won't complete his project by the deadline and sits at his desk doing "worry-work" well in advance, waiting for creative inspiration to strike.

This workaholic behavior goes beyond job- or school-related tasks. The IP Workaholic who is to host a winter holiday party starts planning the menu and decorations in August; the woman who wants to appear attractive at a social event worries for days or weeks in advance about her hair, clothes, and makeup.

IP Workaholics must approach projects or situations in this way because they see every performance event as being crucial. Whether it be a report, a test, or a dinner party, this event holds the potential to be "the big one"—the one that will expose them as frauds to the very people they want to impress.

Paige, a corporate consultant, described this feeling. "I always feel like I have to master every part of my job," she said. "If I'm going on a client call, I'll prepare for four hours. Whereas somebody else might not prepare at all; they might just go there and listen to what the client has to say. I always try to go in with some kind of script, because I'm afraid if they ask me a question and I don't know the answer to it, they'll automatically think I'm an idiot."

IP Workaholics typically achieve success in what they set out to do because they are talented and competent. The department head receives praise for the report and a new program is initiated on the basis of his suggestions; the student gets an A; the host or hostess is recognized as having given the best party of the season.

However, any enjoyment of that success is short-lived. Workaholic IP victims can't relax and savor their rewards. Almost immediately, they begin to worry about the *next* performance event. They wonder whether they can sustain the successful image of themselves they have created. No one found them out *this time*. But maybe the next one will be "the big one." Perhaps they won't be able to put out such superhuman efforts time and time again.

Every task is given equal weight in the mind of an IP Workaholic. They never experiment with their level of effort, or "slack off" to any degree. And, since they don't vary their workaholic behavior, they can't see that it isn't necessary to labor so hard *every time* on *everything* to remain successful. Therefore, they view their success as being due primarily, or disproportionately, to hard work—rather than ability, talent, intelligence, or creativity.

IP Workaholics are caught up in a vicious circle. They observe that their Herculean efforts and constant overwork are always followed by success. This is the point at which the cognitive, or thinking, component of their pattern comes into play. They tend to think that they must not be very competent or talented *because they have to work so hard to achieve*. They make the assumption that they couldn't have attained their success without those unwavering, intensive efforts.

"I guess I've gotten where I am today mainly through hard work and charm," explained Sara, a thirty-eight-year-old speech therapist. "All the women in my family have been hard workers, especially my mother. The men have always been coddled; the women always took care of things. I was expected to be strong like them and a hard worker too. So I'm used to working hard. I've done it all my life. But I sometimes think: 'Well, if I were *really* bright, then I wouldn't have to work this hard.'

"I guess I keep on working so hard because everything is based on that. I'm afraid to stop, because it's like the domino theory—if I stop, then the whole system collapses."

IP Workaholics often refer to themselves as "overachievers." This implies that they have attained a measure of success that exceeds their natural aptitudes—simply by working harder than everybody else.

In Chapter 1, I mentioned a study conducted by Jeanne Stahl and her colleagues of 41 black female high-school science majors. The study had found that 55 percent of these young women believed their achievements were primarily the result of some factor other than intelligence (such as hard work and perseverance).

When the researchers asked them if they felt their teachers or parents ever overestimated their intellectual abilities, 79 percent said their teachers had done so, and 68 percent stated their parents had. "Clearly," wrote Stahl and her fellow researchers, "these women believe that they are overachievers, that their performance is a result of hard work and luck, rather than the intelligence which others may attribute to them."[2]

To understand the IP Workaholic pattern, it is helpful to think about psychologist Harold H. Kelley's "principle of covariation."[3] His principle states that people use the same method as scientists do to determine whether or not their explanations of cause and effect for an event are correct. A scientist varies experimental conditions to see if a certain effect will always occur. In the same way, most people systematically vary situations in order to see what leads to what.

We can see how this principle applies to our own lives. Perhaps a public speaker sometimes reads from extensive notes and sometimes speaks extemporaneously; if he is always well-received, he becomes more certain that a genuine talent for public speaking leads to the applause. A hostess might prepare simple meals on some occasions and elaborate dinners on others; if she finds that guests enjoy being in her home in both cases, she grows increasingly confident of her skills at entertaining. A student might burn the midnight oil some of the time, but feel the need to "goof off" once in a while; if he consistently earns high marks, he grows more confident of his natural intelligence.

IP Workaholics, on the other hand, don't follow this

natural tendency to vary situations. They fail to act like good scientists. Instead, they prepare for *every* public speaking occasion with detailed notes, *every* dinner party with elaborate menus, *every* exam with exhaustive studying. They can't bring themselves to change their behavior and see what would happen.

The result is, they discount the importance of their natural gifts as the cause of their achievements. At the same time, they overinflate the significance of their relentless toiling. We all know that hard work is one important factor in success. But in the mind of an IP Workaholic, hard work is the *only* factor. He fails to recognize that hard work *by itself* couldn't sustain his successes over time. With his unvarying, driven work habits, he is unknowingly preventing himself from discovering the part that ability, competence, and talent play in his achievements.

THE MAGICAL THINKER

Some IP Workaholics are also Magical Thinkers. But anyone else can fit into this pattern as well.

Magical thinking is a term psychologists typically use to refer to some people's belief that their thoughts can affect reality. This type of thinking doesn't follow the process of logic; instead, an individual hopes (or fears) that he can alter what happens simply by what he thinks.

For IP victims, magical thinking takes the shape of constant, ritualistic worrying about performance. The IP Magical Thinker has intense, repeated visions of failure as he prepares for the task at hand.

Because they are often naturally gifted, these IP victims usually do well in the end. But the worrying ritual has become linked in their minds to success; they dare not violate it. They fear that if they allowed optimistic thoughts of success to surface, then they might actually fail. They start to feel that worrying is protecting them from failing.

IP Magical Thinkers always maintain a pessimistic attitude about future success. The lawyer prepares his case with visions of the opposing side exposing the weaknesses in his argument. While preparing his application for a grant, the scientist imagines being turned down. When the boss assigns her a new project, the executive immediately anticipates doing a poor job on it. The man or woman asking for a date visualizes this request being met by humiliating rejection.

This worrying becomes a ritual that precedes every performance event for the Magical Thinker. Anxious dread interferes with any enjoyment of his preparations. Optimism about success is forbidden to him.

Every month, Anna has to write a report for her boss, and "every single month I have the sense I can't do it this time," she said. "I did it last time, but I don't know how. Each one has been better than the last, but it doesn't get any easier, it gets harder. I think: 'The last ones were lucky. Now you're not going to be able to do it.' The same thing happens when I'm beginning *anything*."

Kerry is an interior designer in Boston who specializes in redecorating offices. Even though her clients have always been satisfied with her work, she begins every job with the expectation that it will reveal her lack of talent.

"I've never started a job without the fear of failing at it," she said. "I get superstitious. When I'm driving along, I tell myself, 'If this light at the corner doesn't change before I get there, it will be okay, they won't hate everything I've picked.' I try to reassure myself that I won't get thrown out, or if it's not okay, it won't be a disaster, or it won't necessarily be my fault. It scares me."

Intellectually, the Magical Thinker knows that worrying is not the real cause of his achievements. Emotionally, however, he believes that if he should ever anticipate doing well, fate would punish him by taking away his success. The ritual *appears* to be working for him. Why abandon a sure thing?

The IP Magical Thinker shows some of the same obsessional characteristics described by UCLA psychologist David Shapiro in his work on personality and character styles. In his book *Autonomy and Rigid Character*,[4] Shapiro explains how some obsessional people consciously force themselves, through an act of will, to worry about the worst possible disasters that could befall them. As Shapiro writes about this type of person: "Any other attitude seems to him irresponsible and careless, inviting trouble by its nonchalance or—as one such person put it—'living in a fool's paradise.'"

Shapiro goes on to describe ritualistic worrying as "an effect of a dutiful and coercive will exercised here in the forcing of oneself, again and again, to imagine the worst, not to shrink from it, to exhaust all its possibilities. It may be said, in fact, that for some people worrying can be as driven and obligatory as work is for others."

Shapiro makes another point about some obsessive people that applies as well to IP Magical Thinkers. He notes that these individuals cannot *completely* believe in the disasters they fear. For if they did, they would behave differently, taking more realistic precautions. As he observes, the person who worries about the loss of his job doesn't actually start looking for another one. This type of person, writes Shapiro, "does not completely believe in the likelihood of disaster; but as a person of special conscientiousness he cannot dismiss or take the possibility lightly either." So it is for the IP Magical Thinker.

Superstition and ritual are certainly nothing new. They can be traced throughout history in different cultures. Many of us have our own private forms of ritual. Maybe you have a "morning ritual" to prepare for the day ahead (first the coffee, *then* the shower; never the other way around).

Further, many of us believe, or at least go along with, some forms of superstition. We accept the fact that buildings are designed "without" a thirteenth floor because the number thirteen is thought to bring bad luck. I wonder how many adults, given a choice, would walk around a ladder rather than under it—just to be on the safe side. And once we've uttered the words, how many of us can resist carrying out the ritual that accompanies the expression "Knock on wood"?

In psychoanalytic theory, superstitious thinking is viewed as a remnant from childhood, as well as from primitive times. Remember the old rhyme "Step on a crack, break your mother's back"? This is one example of a ritual from childhood. The child knows intellectually that avoiding the sidewalk cracks won't really protect his mother from injury. Yet, emotionally, there is a driven need to carry out this nonproductive ritual.

For a child, these kinds of rituals are often a way of denying his own feelings of aggression, envy, jealousy, and hostility. Sometimes, when a child avoids the cracks to "protect" his mother, he is playing out the idea of protecting her against what is really his own unconscious wish to hurt her. It is very frightening for a child to realize that he has such feelings and can't handle them on a conscious level. Rituals are one means of coping with them.

The IP Magical Thinker is also driven by the need to engage in a ritual—in this case, to worry. The worrying serves no constructive purpose; it won't help one to hold a job or close an important sale. Yet the Magical Thinker fears the consequences of violating the worry ritual. Superstition is at work here on an emotional level, no matter how sharp the person's intellect may be.

THE SHRINKING VIOLET

"Shrinking Violet" is a term I use to describe certain IP sufferers who are extremely modest, unassuming, and reluctant to accept compliments. If they should receive praise—be it for their work, talent, intellect, beauty, sense of style, or concern for others—their natural tendency is to resist it. They have great difficulty in responding with a simple "Thank you" and letting it go at that. Instead, they feel compelled to point out minor flaws in what they have done, subtle touches they have missed, or ways in which they could strive for improvement. They often contrast themselves with others who are "really" bright, creative, beautiful, altruistic, etc.

"Whether they're complimenting me on my work, my appearance, or my new shoes, I say, 'Oh no, not really,' " related one woman. "I get shy and bow my little head. I never say, 'Thank you, you're right.' "

In some cases, Shrinking Violets have found through experience that it is socially inappropriate to deny compliments, because it makes the person offering the compliment feel awkward. They may manage to say "Thank you" and then keep quiet. But it is a supreme struggle to suppress that urge to refute the compliment. So even if they are able to accept praise graciously in public, privately they still deny it.

"Originally I had a hard time accepting compliments," one man told me. "I thought my work was never as good as it could have been, and I can see the faults with a little distance. I ask myself, 'Why couldn't I have seen that when I was doing it?' But now I just *say,* 'Thank you.' "

Deep inside, the Shrinking Violet feels that any display of pride on his part will eventually be punished by some humiliating failure. He may fear that other people will become so jealous of him, they will start waiting for the day they can vengefully rejoice at his exposure as mediocre or incompetent. His humility and modesty are ways of defending himself against the exposure he fears. "Blessed are the meek" is this person's unconscious motto.

IP Shrinking Violets often suffer from a profound fear that others will think they are arrogant. And they fear the penalties for arrogance. They believe that if they act too proud, others will ostracize them socially, talk about them behind their back, or start to compete with them. By denying compliments or praise, they hope they are protecting themselves from acting, or being seen as, arrogant.

Shrinking Violets fear that acknowledging and accepting praise will make them more visible and only hasten their eventual downfall. But if you can't internalize praise, you can't use it to build a self-concept that includes the image of success. Denying praise and positive feedback enhances self-doubt instead of self-confidence.

Inside, these people may react to compliments in a variety of ways. They may feel anxiety, embarrassment, or suspicion toward the person offering the compliment. Or assume the other person simply doesn't realize their achievements were a matter of pure good luck. Some people feel that unqualified praise isn't to be believed; the praise doesn't seem valid unless some criticism comes along with it.

"When someone praises my work, I cringe and wonder what they want," said Melissa, a research associate in a science lab. "Are they buttering me up, getting ready to go in for the kill and really tear it apart? Or are they just telling me my work is good because there's no other sucker around to dump the next load of shitwork on? On the outside, I've stopped 'taking away their compliments' for fear that they will catch on that I'm not sure my work is good."

Some people do feel, on one level, that they deserve some praise and recognition. Yet when it comes, they can't quite accept it.

An associate at a law firm, Jessie says she knows she is doing a good job as a lawyer. One day, she had written a legal brief that was highly praised by one of the firm's senior partners. He told the other attorneys that it was one of the best briefs he had ever seen, and he only wished every brief was as well-done. Yet Jessie described her reaction this way: "I *knew* that brief was not good. It wasn't bad, but it was *nothing* compared to what I could do—because it was so easy for me to do. I did it very quickly, and somehow that made it not that good in my eyes. I felt like if it wasn't hard to do, it's not really worth anything, it's not so good. I thought, 'Oh, he just likes me' and 'That poor guy—he's never seen a good brief in his life.' "

Shrinking Violets will go to any lengths to resist compliments. They deny the objective evidence of their competence in several ways: denigrating the value of their performance, exaggerating the flaws, dissociating themselves from any credit for what they've done, devaluing the opinions of those experts who praise them. The people who follow this pattern seldom fully understand the reasons behind their behavior. In fact, the urge to deny compliments is often related to an unconscious need. It is intended to ward off public recognition and the penalties someone may fear for being recognized as successful.

*　　*　　*

THE CHARMER

The IP Charmer tends to be a high achiever who is attractive, likable, socially adept, witty, warm, and, in some cases, flirtatious. His personality assets help to make an appealing, positive impression on others. People enjoy spending time in his company.

These individuals have usually possessed the same personality assets since childhood. In high school, they were well-liked and popular—probably president of the student council, a cheerleader, or a school athlete. They have always gotten along well with others. In the area of social skills, they rate very high.

Of course, not everyone who is charming believes he is a fake. What distinguishes the Charmer IP victim is the way he *thinks* about his own social skills.

Charmers think they are "getting by" on their charm, or getting ahead *because* of charm rather than their "true" abilities. It is their charm, they believe, that wins them business connections, work and/or friends. They fear that without their social skills, the work would stop coming and their friends might abandon them. Yet they have mixed feelings about the part these skills play in their success. Charmers often refer to themselves as having a certain "flair" or "style," suggesting that this is concealing some lack of underlying substance.

Lucy is an import agent who had always been known in her family as the "personality kid." As an adult, she is aware that her social skills appear to play a part in making important business contacts and cementing deals for her company. Yet, she is very uncertain about the value of these skills, questioning whether they are talents that "really count."

"When you're in a business where people see you only once or twice a year," she reflected, "personality *is* a key factor in success. But even though I know this,

I still feel my charm is worthless and slightly sickening."

Lucy sees her ability to charm people as a form of manipulation. "It's just getting people to do what you want. I guess I have a tendency to undervalue the things I'm good at, and overvalue the things I have more concern about. It's so easy, I feel like it must not be right, it must not be a skill."

Even though she doubts the validity of her charm as a skill or talent, Lucy believes that it is covering up her lack of ability to handle her work. "I think in business you probably have to be the kind of person somebody wants to work with. But if you base your whole career on personality and charm—if you have any failings in that area, it's a very frightening thing. The people who I think are bad bosses are bad because they're only doing it based on personality. You do have to be a knowledgeable person with something significant to contribute.

"Sometimes I sit in my office with something that I really have to get done, and I think, 'I'll never finish this and I'll get in trouble.' And people will reevaluate me and that will be the beginning of the end."

If you have always been personable and popular, *and* successful professionally, you can reach one of two conclusions about the cause-and-effect relationship between your achievements and your personal charm.

If you don't feel like an impostor, you might tell yourself that personality may have been helpful in making important contacts, or in initially getting hired for a project or job. You would assume, however, that over the long run your reputation was built upon the quality of your work. You are a qualified, talented, able person who produces results time and time again—and happens to be charming as well. And, in truth, few employers or clients are so swayed by charm that they will continue to employ someone who can't produce what is needed. They couldn't afford it.

On the other hand, if you are a warm, charming person who experiences "impostor" feelings, you probably don't see it this way. You may worry that your social skills have blinded others to your short-comings. This is the thinking, or cognitive, part of this pattern.

The dilemma arises because IP Charmers believe that their personal attractiveness and likability create a sort of "halo" effect that clouds even the judgment of experts. When their work is praised and considered successful, their basic doubts about their talents and abilities surface. Any praise they receive is immediately disowned and devalued as an overestimate based on false premises.

The Charmer's thought process prevents him from accepting and internalizing praise. The positive feedback that could be self-enhancing falls, in effect, on deaf ears. And so the cycle persists.

Though a Charmer IP victim can be male or female, there are some aspects to this pattern that are of particular concern for women.

It is no secret to anyone that our culture places a high value on physical attractiveness in women. As a result, many women strive toward reaching an ideal of beauty. From adolescence, or even earlier, they may have invested a great deal of time and money in the effort to become more attractive.

In addition, although social attitudes are changing, many women have grown up believing that they must not be too aggressive, or they run the risk of becoming unfeminine and undesirable in the eyes of men. Instead, they have been taught (directly or indirectly) that they should use charm to get what they want.

It's not surprising that some women who attempt to meet these standards may feel that the way they look and act is, in some sense, fraudulent. They may see themselves as faking it, playing a part, not showing or expressing "the real me." The fact that they feel at odds with behavior they have been taught is "correct" and desirable for a woman only adds to the guilt and confusion.

This can be an especially thorny area for business-women suffering from the Impostor Phenomenon. The attractive, personable female employee may wonder if her promotions are based on her charm, looks, or sexuality, rather than on the merit of her work. More than one woman has told me that at times she did indeed feel her business opportunities or promotions were due to her charm and attractiveness.

This is a double-edged sword. If a woman credits all her achievements to such qualities, she is ignoring the fact that talent and ability are required for success. And if she chooses to tone down her good looks or personal warmth to insure that she avoids the question altogether, she is depriving herself of her own natural assets.

Getting caught up in this dilemma can create serious problems for attractive, talented women who attempt to use the male mentor system on their road to achievement (and for young men who may find female mentors).

Take, for example, the female graduate school stu-dent who tries to gain the time and special attention of a male professor. In graduate school, the time of the best professors is limited. Students are forced to com-pete for that time in any way they can. Attractive female students may flatter, entertain, flirt, or joke with their professors, possibly arousing the envy of other students who don't possess those same good looks or social skills.

Charm and flirtatiousness may work in getting that special invitation for coffee or lunch. Once alone with the professor, the attractive student can concentrate on getting the professor interested in her research. At the very least, she gets noticed in a highly favorable way, provided her seductiveness is not too blatant (and, sometimes, even when it is).

This doesn't necessarily mean that the student will pass with honors if her academic work is poor. But she has chosen to use certain personality assets to help her gain an edge in a highly competitive situation. A female junior executive might use the same approach to attract the notice and attention of someone in upper management.

For the woman who feels like a fraud, however, this system becomes self-defeating. She may receive the time, attention, and praise she is seeking for her ideas and work. Yet she is never really certain that her charm, looks, or personality have not misled the professor (or boss or mentor) into overestimating her knowledge and intellect.

It's easy to understand why Yvette, an attractive and charming woman who feels she is "trading" on her charm, still remembers one particular incident. She had just completed a job interview in which she had to meet with several people from the company at the same time. She later learned that after she had left the room, one of her interviewers remarked, "We should hire her just because she's so charming."

There are times when a relationship with a boss, professor, or mentor does become romantic or sexual. This relationship doesn't have to be based on manipulation. Usually, the protégée has idealized the other person and truly falls in love, or believes she is in love.

However, for the IP victim, the end result is always the same. She (or he) worries that she is participating in some variation of the old "casting couch" routine. She wonders if her fellow co-workers or students are jealous or scornful of her ("Oh, she slept her way to the top") and are waiting for some fatal misstep that will lead to her humiliation.

She then sets perfectionistic standards for herself, expecting her work to be better than that of her peers and colleagues. She needs to prevent other people—and, mostly, herself—from suspecting that she is doing well simply because of her favored situation in the sexual relationship.

Whether the IP Charmer is a man or a woman, the cognitive part of this pattern is in the person's interpretation of how his social assets have influenced his success. He *knows* he is good at getting along with people and is well-liked, but he questions the value of his natural abilities. Again, he doesn't act like a good scientist: He makes an untested assumption, namely, that without his social skills, he wouldn't have accomplished much at all.

THE CHAMELEON

In the movie *Zelig,* Woody Allen portrayed a character who changed his appearance and personality—even his race or nationality—to resemble whomever he was with. By transforming himself to be exactly like other people, Zelig hoped he would be loved and accepted.

I hardly need to point out that, in reality, no one can magically change himself to the extent that Zelig did. But some people who feel they are impostors take this same sort of approach. To win the approval of others, they suppress their own personalities and take on the personality of someone else.

These are the people I describe as IP Chameleons. Like the lizards who change their skin color to blend in with their surroundings, they adapt to situations that make them anxious by "blending in" with other people's personalities. They become like the other person, agreeing with his views and attitudes. If an IP Chameleon seeks the approval of someone in particular, he may go as far as copying that person's style of dress, or taking up his hobby.

By becoming just like the person he is with, this IP victim is protecting himself. He creates a camouflage to hide his imperfections—imperfections that he fears are fatal flaws. This way, no one can expose him as the incompetent or unintelligent person he thinks he really is.

Joyce is a product manager for a packaged-goods company. She herself described her style of dealing with people as "somewhat chameleonlike." "I do tend to get along with people," she said. "I figure out on some superficial level what they're like, and be like that enough so that we get along okay.

"I listen to people a lot; I probably talk less than other people. I'm less authoritative in my opinions. I try to listen to what everybody else is saying and consider that. I think I manipulate people to a certain extent by listening. I've won a lot of battles by just letting it go on—just listening, listening, nodding and nodding. After a while, they get tired and just stop! If you don't say a whole lot, they think you really know. You haven't revealed any ignorance. It's my experience that people who talk a lot reveal just how ignorant they are, and with those who manage to keep quiet, nobody's ever quite sure."

If they disagree with the person whose approval they desire, Chameleons will ignore their inner voice and outwardly express agreement. Or, they may choose simply to remain silent.

Think about the executive sitting in a large meeting. If he is a Chameleon IP type, he is not likely to speak up when his opinion conflicts with that of the department head or boss. Even though his position is well thought-out, he is afraid to voice it. As he reasons: "If I disagree with my boss, I could well be wrong.

Everyone will see the flaw that *I* can't see in my position, and I'll be exposed as stupid. Besides, if I disagree, my boss won't like me.''

What often happens is that someone else in the room—someone who doesn't feel like an impostor—"scoops" the Chameleon. The other person expresses the same thought while the Chameleon is vacillating over whether or not to speak. That person then gets the credit for an interesting, well-analyzed argument.

There are many times when it is practical and realistic to agree with the boss, no matter what we may be thinking. Yet an employee can also promote his usefulness by contributing ideas, even by helping the boss realize he may be making an error. Some people, though, can't take the risk of disagreeing with a superior. They are afraid that they will make him feel threatened and incur his disapproval. Or, some might think: "Maybe the boss will actually use my idea or do this project my way. Then, when things go wrong, I'll be blamed and humiliated. The boss and everyone else will know my idea was dumb and they should never have listened to me."

Chameleons are often highly vocal and visible in promoting someone else's cause. They are good disciples and faithful followers, sometimes virtual carbon copies of those whom they admire.

At thirty-nine, Francine is the first woman to have reached the management level in sales at her Cleveland-based company. She talks about how, having reached this position in business, she began to take on the values (the "colors," as she calls them) of her male colleagues.

"I adapted to them," Francine explained. "At first, I would go out drinking on Friday nights with the boys. I just kind of molded into it at first, and it didn't feel that alien to me because I'm a party person and I like people. That was fine at first. But you reach a level where you *have to* do that, where it's expected of you. It's part of the milieu and you just go with it. If you don't, don't bother showing up."

Over time, she observed, "I found that I was getting more and more like them. And my friends—old friends, people I'd known since I started this job—have been commenting about the changes they've seen in me that I know are real. The hardness, the cynicism. I've always had a good sense of humor, but now there's an edge to it, a bite."

In personal roles outside the office, the Chameleon's compliant behavior often involves a fear of expressing anger. Some Chameleons feel that if they disagree or argue with a friend, they run the risk of permanently losing the friendship. They believe personal rejection will result because they have been a "bad" friend. The woman who doubts whether she is a "good" wife may feel that her role demands that she publicly agree with her husband, or at least keep silent, even when her own views conflict with his. Of course, secretly she knows her own opinions differ—which gives rise to an inner sense of fraudulence.

The cognitive, or thinking, aspect of this pattern makes it an especially difficult one to break. It's true that the Chameleon IP victim does practice a certain amount of inauthentic, "phony" behavior. He is consciously aware that he is adopting attitudes of voicing opinions not his own. This provides the grain of truth to his sense of fraudulence. But, as he observes himself acting inauthentic, he wrongly concludes that if he were truly intelligent, competent, or "good," he wouldn't have to behave this way.

IP Chameleons need to understand that their tactics of "blending in"—agreeing, accommodating, keeping silent—are not evidence of incompetence, but are methods they have chosen to cope with their anxieties. These IP victims "change their colors" as a protective camouflage. They want to shield themselves from those things they dread: exposure, rejection, and personal attack. Their coping methods are designed as defenses against anticipated hostility and criticism from others, as well as self-criticism.

In truth, such methods are inefficient. The pattern of behavior itself creates more anxiety and self-blame for them than would disagreement, self-expression, and promotion of their own opinions and values.

THE GENIE

As the story goes, if you rub Aladdin's lamp, a genie will appear and grant your wishes. The IP victims whom I call Genies also grant wishes—but they are psychological wishes, rather than material ones.

These people are gifted with a highly developed sense of intuition and a strong sensitivity to the needs of others. They are adept at discovering even the most subtle psychological needs of those whose approval they seek. Unlike IP Chameleons, who mimic someone else, Genies zero in on what another person would like them to be and become exactly that.

Although you would have to *tell* Aladdin's genie what you want, IP Genies can discern your wish without your having to express it directly. It's almost as if they had a special sort of ESP that enables them to know what others need, comparable to a mother sensing the needs of her newborn infant.

Once they have figured out what the person in question needs or desires—and they can do this very quickly—Genies set out to supply it. Psychologists would say they behave in complementarity, meaning that they intuit and then provide whatever it is the "significant other" is missing. They *become* whatever will fill that person's need, or "complement" that person.

Take, for example, the IP Genie seeking approval

from a new boss at work. He will sense intuitively what qualities this person responds to and gain his attention by emphasizing those qualities in himself. If the boss is looking for someone who will challenge him rather than echo his views, the Genie disdains simple "yessing" and wins over the boss with challenges. The boss feels that he is misunderstood at home? The Genie is ready with a warm shoulder and sympathetic ear. Perhaps the boss responds to intellectual stimulation; in that case, the Genie initiates intellectually provocative conversations.

"I sort of feel out the way someone is right away," said Ross, an art director. "I have a tendency to try to be the kind of person I know that person would like. So if I sense that person likes someone who is calm, I'll try and fit into that mold. I become a very flexible person. And then I begin to doubt who I am because I fit into so many different molds. Some people like me to be funnier, so I become more entertaining. Other people like me to be efficient, so I do that. I definitely try to provide whatever it is they want in terms of personality. And then the actual work that I'm doing seems secondary."

In some cases, a Genie may respond to the sexual needs of someone whose approval he craves. Or, he may pick up on someone else's desire for plain warmth and affection. I asked one IP sufferer what she was best at when she was trying to decide what career path to follow. She was a gifted, attractive, young black woman with great intelligence and numerous talents. Her response caught me off-guard. She told me: "I'm very good at love. I figure out what the people I care about need, and I give it to them."

Here is how Colleen, a financial analyst, explained the way she interacts with people: "I've sometimes felt I have this uncanny ability to know exactly what to say to make the situation right—to move it in the direction that makes me comfortable, and also makes the other person think that it's where they want to be. Even as a child I had this sense of being this horribly precocious adult. I could always maneuver things in the direction that made everybody think things were going well."

In personal roles as well, there are all types of situations in which people who believe that they are frauds engage in Genielike behavior as they search for some sort of validation. The mother suffering from "impostor" feelings may try to provide for her child's every need, anticipating requests before the child has even voiced them; she is seeking validation of her self-image as a "good mother." Someone else may sense and fulfill a lover's every wish to prevent that person from ever experiencing frustration or dissatisfaction; he hopes to find validation of a self-image as the perfect lover who is all things to the one he adores. The person who spends hours agonizing over the perfect gift for a friend's birthday wants reassurance that he fits an idealized image of what a good friend should be.

Whether the Genie is dealing with a boss, mentor, client, friend, or lover, he sees his function as that of gratifying the other's needs. At first glance, then, it would appear that he pushes aside his own needs. But, in fact, his behavior is really geared to winning him approval in some area. Unfortunately, like the other IP patterns, this habit of behavior is self-defeating. It doesn't lead to the desired goal.

As Clance and Imes have noted, certain IP victims who set out to satisfy the needs of mentors in business are really longing for the mentor to validate their ability, talent, and intelligence. They are looking for a stamp of approval, so to speak. Yet, when the praise and admiration are finally won, IP victims can't really believe it. They think it must be due to what they see as their manipulations, rather than having been deserved on its own merit.[5]

In observing himself, the Genie IP victim finds that he is in a no-win situation. If the appreciation and admiration he longs for are not forthcoming, he loses his sense of "specialness," because he hasn't lived up to some ideal. What has happened is that he has allowed his self-image in a particular role to be determined by someone else's reaction—or lack of one—to him. In this case, his self-doubt surfaces, and he begins to think, "I'm really not very bright or talented (or a good mother, good lover, or good friend)."

On the other hand, when praise, appreciation, and love are expressed by the recipients of his "wish-granting," the Genie interprets these rewards as the result of insincere manipulations, instead of as evidence of his worth. His most common reaction is doubt. "Do they really appreciate, admire, or love me for *myself*," he wonders, "or just because I make myself into whatever they want?" Once again, an IP pattern only serves to reinforce self-doubt.

Feeling Like a Fake in Your Personal Life

THREE

When you were growing up you suspected that everyone else had been let in on some fundamental secret which was kept from you. Others seemed to know what they were doing. This conviction grew with each new school you attended. Your father's annual job transfers made you the perennial new kid. Every year there was a new body of lore to be mastered. The color of your bike, your socks, was always wrong. . . . Not until you reached college, where everyone started fresh, did you begin to pick up the tricks of winning friends and influencing people. Although you became adept, you also felt that you were exercising an acquired skill, something that came naturally to others. You succeeded in faking everyone out, and never quite lost the fear that you would eventually be discovered a fraud, an impostor in the social circle.

—From the novel Bright Lights, Big City *by Jay McInerney*

Up until now, we have been looking at the Impostor Phenomenon primarily in relation to the roles that people play in their work or studies. It was in this light that the IP initially revealed itself to psychologists. We heard people talk about feeling fraudulent in connection with their careers or academic pursuits. We conducted studies of this phenomenon focusing on people in their jobs. The workplace was the arena in which we identified and came to understand the Impostor Phenomenon.

At the same time, though, I noticed something else happening. My patients and other IP victims were telling me that they felt like fakes in their *personal* lives as well. They were experiencing feelings of phoniness in areas that had nothing to do with their jobs.

They told me of feeling like impostors in their roles as friends. As lovers. As spouses. As parents. As sons or daughters. They said they were impostors as adults—secretly they felt they were only children "pretending" to be grown-ups. They experienced feelings of phoniness in regard to their looks, social skills, family loyalties, love for others, social standing. They questioned the sincerity of their charitable and altruistic acts—even their basic goodness as human beings.

I heard the same phrases other IP victims use about

their work roles: "I'm really not the way I appear to be. I'm faking it. I'm afraid they're going to find out."

It soon became clear to me that the Impostor Phenomenon encompasses far more than the world of work. I believe it's time we psychologists redefine the Impostor Phenomenon to include personal life as well.

To understand the link between the Impostor Phenomenon and personal roles, it is helpful to take another look at what a role actually is. When I talk about a role, I mean the appropriate, expected behavior connected to a person's position or status. We all play many different roles in the course of a single day. Often, without even being aware of it, we switch from one role to another almost automatically. "Playing a role" doesn't mean we are pretending, or acting in a false manner.

If you are a working wife and mother, you probably get up and help your children get ready for school; from 7:00 to 8:00 A.M. you are playing the role of mother. By 9:00 A.M. you are at your desk, playing the role of a businessperson. At 6:00 P.M. you meet your old high-school chum for a drink, and you switch into the role of friend. Dinner at 8:00 with your husband— move into the role of wife.

There is certainly nothing fake or phony about these roles. They are all parts of an individual's identity. Roles help us to impose some order on what might otherwise be chaotic social interactions. And each one contains certain ways of behaving that are appropriate to carrying out that role successfully. You may wear a bathrobe while you're helping the kids get into their snowsuits, but you're going to dress quite differently to go on a sales call with your potential new client.

We play a number of different roles simultaneously. If you and your husband are eating in a restaurant, the two of you are not only playing your roles of husband and wife; you are also assuming the roles of "people eating in a restaurant." You order your food, eat, pay the check, and leave. This is the basic behavior of your role. You don't bring in your own food and silverware, rearrange all the furniture, and wash the dishes after you eat (unless you tried to skip the "pay the check" part of your role).

The problem comes in when someone begins to doubt how well, or how sincerely, he is playing a personal role—even though he appears to others to be doing a good job at it. It is far more difficult to measure success in this area. There are no salaries, no job titles, and no awards to prove that one is doing well. But many people carry images in their minds of how they *should* feel and behave in various roles.

Sometimes we can see that we actually are doing well in a role, or we receive recognition from others that tells us so. Yet our inner feelings conflict with our actions. If we start to doubt our sincerity, we can imagine that we are only faking our way through a part.

Feelings of fraudulence in certain personal roles are typically accompanied by feelings of guilt. Personal roles involve direct interaction with other people, often the people whom we care about the most. If you believe that you are deceiving someone close to you, you probably feel guilty and ashamed about it.

People who suffer from the Impostor Phenomenon in their personal lives usually have one explanation for why they are "successful" as friends, lovers, parents, etc. They don't attribute their success to the same kinds of factors IP victims mention in regard to work. Good luck, hard work, or the right timing don't apply here. When it comes to personal roles, they talk about "putting on a false front." They believe that they are acting in a way that conflicts with how they really feel, with what they're really like, inside.

Not everyone who feels inadequate or guilty in

71

some area of his personal life is a victim of the Impostor Phenomenon. Three things distinguish the person who is suffering from this syndrome in connection to a personal role:

1. He believes his inner feelings or weaknesses are a secret that must be kept hidden.
2. He feels he is acting in a fraudulent way to hide his feelings, which increases his guilt over what he sees as his hypocrisy or insincerity in his role.
3. He fears any situation that might lead to his secret feelings being revealed.

As with "impostor" feelings in work roles, the feeling of being a fake in a personal role varies in intensity from person to person. Some feel it in an ongoing way, others only at certain periods in their lives.

Personal roles involve all types of situations, behavior, and feelings. The role of "daughter," for example, is very different from the role of "friend." To understand how the Impostor Phenomenon can strike in personal roles, we have to look at these roles individually. I have chosen several of the most common roles we play, and the ones that most often seem to bring on feelings of phoniness.

THE IP AND FRIENDSHIP

Many people have told me that they believe they are impostors as friends. They feel a friend should act and feel in a certain way. Even though they *act* the way they're "supposed to," they don't always *feel* the way they think they should about doing it. In their minds, they just don't live up to the image of what a friend should be.

We can come up with a lot of different ideas about what makes an ideal friend. Our image of a friend might be someone who is easy to get along with, always ready to provide warmth and sympathy to others. Or someone who would never refuse to do a favor for another friend in need. We might reason that if we are to be a real friend, we must live up to that image. Our mental picture of what a real friend should be is the standard by which we measure our own success as a friend.

But just as one person feels he is "faking it" in the role of corporate vice president, another person may feel he is a fraud as a friend.

Let's say that it's Saturday afternoon and you have a list of errands to do that's a mile long. As you're walking out the door, a friend calls and asks if you would come shopping to pick out a dress for her to wear to her cousin's wedding. This is the one day of the week you have to yourself and you would rather not go.

If you believe that you are indeed a real friend, you have several alternatives. You can explain that you're sorry, but you just have too much to do. Or you can tell her that you'll see her later, after you've had a chance to take care of your errands and she's checked out a few stores on her own. You might decide to meet her, catch up on your chores next week, and not give the matter a second thought.

This situation is likely to be quite different if the person being asked is worried about whether or not she is a real friend. She answers, "Why, of course, I'd be glad to meet you." She genuinely *wants* to help out her friend and does so with a smile. But, inside, she knows she would rather be attending to her own needs. She begins to feel guilty because her enthusiasm is not one hundred percent sincere. "A truly good friend wouldn't be so selfish," she thinks. "I'm only pretending to be a real friend. I don't even care what she wears to this stupid wedding. What an awful person I must be. I can't let anyone ever find out."

This individual is trying to live up to an idealized image of what a friend should be. Because she isn't *always* happy to help out someone else, she believes she lacks some essential quality in this area. She is convinced that she is an impostor as a friend.

Those people I have heard questioning whether they are "real" or "counterfeit" friends are often the most helpful and considerate friends anyone could ever want. They go out of their way to aid others, to be good listeners, to be available for help with other people's problems at all hours of the day or night.

At times, however, they notice that some of their internal feelings contradict what they're doing on the outside. Their emotions conflict with the behavior that is earning them comments like "Isn't he wonderful?" or "Isn't she just the greatest?"

Renee is a twenty-seven-year-old woman who works as a secretary in a large Southern hospital. The people in her department are a tightly knit group, and she considers them to be close friends. One year, Renee volunteered to organize her department's annual spring picnic. She did such a wonderful job finding the location, handling the logistics, and planning all the food that her co-workers asked her to do it again the following spring.

She gained the reputation of someone who would go out of her way for her friends, reminding them in a warm, encouraging way of what they were to bring or contribute—and doing it herself at the last minute if they were too busy or forgot. Everyone had such a good time at these picnics, they began to rely on her for this service every year.

Renee enjoyed the admiration she received from her co-workers, but her resentment began to build over the idea that they were taking her for granted. Each year she undertook to organize the outing—yet her pleasure in doing so lessened, while her hostility grew. This drained her energy, and made her tired and depressed.

Still, Renee continued to take on this job every year. She was afraid to say no, or to delegate it to someone else, because she thought people would then find out that she wasn't really the good friend they thought her to be. She wanted to prevent others from seeing what she feared was "evidence" that she was selfish, angry, and hypocritical. She was unable to tolerate those negative feelings in herself that seemed to imply she wasn't a real friend.

Renee ignored the overwhelming fact of all the work she had put in for her friends over the years. She gave more weight to how she *felt* than to what she had actually *done*. Because her feelings weren't completely positive ones, she kept them secret and they festered. And because *she* discounted all she had done for her co-workers over the years, she was certain that they would, too. She feared that once they discovered her negative feelings, they would decide that she was no real friend after all.

Thirty-three-year-old Celia loved to travel with her friend Amy. The two had been taking vacation trips together since their college days in New England. After school, they both settled down in Amy's hometown of Seattle. As the years passed and they earned larger salaries, they were able to take more expensive and exotic trips—skiing in Switzerland, visiting Japan and India.

Celia was always the one who planned these trips, because Amy didn't like the process of conferring with travel agents and booking reservations. Celia would spend several months organizing their annual excursions. At first, she enjoyed immersing herself in the planning. She liked talking and reading about the place they had chosen, looking up restaurants they could try, and ferreting out the bargain shops. It was a way of extending the pleasure of the trip itself over a longer period of time.

One year, Celia had been working particularly hard for several months and was exhausted. She wasn't feeling very enthusiastic about their trip, and would have liked Amy to take over the planning stages. But Amy had come to rely on Celia for this. She didn't volunteer and Celia didn't ask. Celia began organizing the trip herself, but instead of feeling her usual enthusiasm and pleasure, she now felt anger and hostility toward her friend for not helping her.

Finally, she found the perfect place at the perfect price—but the package required that they make the trip within the next month. Amy announced she couldn't go away that soon because her brother had been ill and she wanted to stick close to home in case there was a problem with his recovery.

Celia was angry, then depressed. She felt caught in the trap of her mixed emotions. She feared that if she expressed her resentment and disappointment to Amy, her friend would see her for the selfish, "spoiled brat" she felt herself to be. Then Amy would no longer think of her as a "true" friend, but as a mere impostor, a woman who secretly wanted her own way and couldn't compromise for others.

Celia decided not to take the trip at all. All she said to Amy was that they should postpone it until her brother was completely well.

Feelings of resentment such as those experienced by Renee and Celia are troublesome, but certainly not abnormal. However, IP victims reach a different conclusion when they experience mixed feelings, or any discrepancy between their internal feelings and the

76

recognition they receive for their public behavior. They tend to interpret that discrepancy as evidence that they are hypocrites or "phony" friends, despite the high opinion others may hold of them. They expect themselves to be perfect as friends all the time, both inwardly *and* outwardly.

Thirty-six years old, Lloyd is a California psychologist who describes himself as "a very nice guy," a man who can be counted on. "But I'm probably more accommodating than is necessary, and sometimes more than I really want to be," he said. "I'm probably as well-loved as I feel I am because I'm sort of special in a way. If I were as moody or inconsistent, or as selfish at times, as I think the run-of-the-mill guy is, then *I* would be run-of-the-mill, and the affection and respect I enjoy would evaporate."

Lloyd understood what it has meant to him to maintain this image of himself as a reliable, accommodating friend—and why he would be reluctant to give it up.

"On a gut level," he explained, "it's my investment in my image of myself. I have a tremendous investment in being 'special.' And I think my friends and peers pretty much see me that way. That's the thing that I'm most afraid would be compromised. I'm afraid that my perception of my being very well-loved and respected would fade away. I don't *really* think that would happen, but at some level I *feel* that would happen. That's the crux of my fear of being found out."

Like Lloyd, many people feel that preserving this image of an ideal friend means that they can continue to feel special. They fear losing that sense of specialness if they ever disappoint anyone, or if they aren't available, accommodating, and perfectly helpful to their friends all the time. Lloyd has been able to modify this over the years, to learn that saying no doesn't have to mean that he is a bad friend. It will not cause the loss of love, admiration, and respect. Renee and Celia both felt they had to be perfect friends at all times or their "flaws" would become apparent. To them, that meant they would lose their reputations as good friends, and be rejected and ostracized.

We can see from these examples how the Impostor Phenomenon operates in the world of personal roles much as it does in work roles. People who are IP victims in personal roles, like that of friend, have been publicly recognized as "well-qualified" for their roles. They feel a certain pressure to maintain their reputations as successful.

Paulette describes how she was known as "the great listener" in college. Friends always came to her to talk about their problems. "I used to be everything everybody wanted me to be—and they wanted me to listen," she recalled. "After a while, it got to the point where I really wasn't listening to anybody. I was just sitting there, faking listening." Despite her inclinations, Paulette kept doing what people expected her to do (like the IP Genie described in Chapter 2). She maintained the appearance of giving them what they needed.

Many "listeners" began this pattern in childhood. Even in their families, they were known for being understanding without being intrusive. They were quietly empathic, helping others to express their thoughts and find solutions to their problems. They became known as the kind of friend to whom others could come with a problem.

As they grew older, this trait became an important part of their images of themselves as friends. They hesitated to modify it in any way. It made them feel unique, needed, loved, "special." A "listener" could also be described as a nurturing caretaker, helping others to grow without interfering. And some listeners did play a caretaking role for their younger sisters and brothers, perhaps even for a parent.

Sometimes, these individuals long to be the one who is listened *to*. However, that wish causes an internal conflict. At some level, they fear losing their special role if they become "takers" instead of "givers." So they tend to stick with their more familiar part of listener, denying themselves the comfort of allowing someone else to do the same for them.

This ultimately leads to feelings of deprivation and resentment. Yet the IP victim feels he must preserve the "listener" image at all costs in order to maintain his reputation as a good friend. If he isn't offering his wholehearted attention all the time (which is pretty much impossible), he feels phony about the reputation that is so important to him.

Some friends are known more as advice-givers. They are the people to whom others come for counsel in times of trouble or personal conflict. This reputation is also a difficult one to sustain, for who can be that wise all the time? Such a person may want to maintain his reputation as a "wise old owl" because this is what friends have come to expect. But he feels fraudulent because he believes he isn't all that sure about how to handle everyone's problems.

One man put it this way: "Sometimes you become a person who people come to for advice, and, latching on to your own insecurities, you can feel fraudulent about that. Why are all these people asking me? I'm not really sure I know. What makes *me* so knowledgeable?"

Another side of the IP in friendship is believing that you appear to be a better friend than you actually want to be. Sometimes a person becomes involved in a relationship in which his affections are weaker or more ambivalent than the other person's affections are toward him. He may feel that he is an impostor who is only pretending to share an equal interest in maintaining the friendship. In reality, he may not be terribly concerned about holding on to the friendship, or may value only one aspect of it. Perhaps, for example, his friend has a good sense of humor and can always be counted on for a laugh.

The person in this position must make a decision about what this relationship means to him. He is behaving in a slightly "phony" way by trying outwardly to match his friend's level of affection and pretending he cares more than he does. This makes him feel guilty about "being" a fraud. Yet his motive is to avoid hurting the other person's feelings. If he cared nothing at all for his friend, he wouldn't bother to go to all this effort.

There is nothing inherently right or wrong about being friends with someone who cares more for you than you do for him. Relationships aren't divided up measure for measure. The reality is that we don't like everybody in the same way or to the same extent. Another point: Unless the other person is actually masochistic, he is getting something out of this friendship. You simply might not know what that is. After all, he's a free agent who can walk away from the situation any time he wants.

THE IP AND LOVE

Romantic love, whether in or out of marriage, is another area where one can be vulnerable to "impostor" feelings. Some people have revealed to me that at times they feel fraudulent about the quality of their love for others. They doubt its sincerity. This is particularly true for those who strive to love so well and so perfectly that they intuitively sense the needs of the loved one, and make themselves into whatever will fill those needs.

Perhaps this idea is most evident when two people first fall in love. In a new romantic situation, most people will strive to put their best foot forward and make a good impression. Of course, IP victims do this as well—but they interpret it as acting fraudulent.

At times, people in love also experience some conflicting feelings toward each other. They might become annoyed over small things ("Must you *always* leave the bathroom looking like a cyclone hit it?") or occasionally have doubts over whether they want to stay with the other person. IP victims often interpret those feelings as proof that their love is not "real." Yet their outward behavior and long-term loving feelings show strong evidence of their devotion. In fact, their love may be real, but not perfect or ideal.

As we've seen, those who suffer from the Impostor Phenomenon tend to be very much aware of contradictions between their thoughts and actions. And they want to live up to an idealized image. It is difficult for them to tolerate anything short of perfection from themselves, and they typically focus in on the one issue that would make them feel counterfeit. Love that contains a "flaw" is seen as less than perfect. An IP victim magnifies that flaw to the extent that he begins to doubt the reality of his love, and wonders whether it is just an illusion that is fooling others.

In addition to perfectionism, there may be a second aspect to a relationship that makes someone doubt the quality of his love. People involved in deep love relationships are often sensitive to their partner's needs, and feel a desire to nurture the other person and help them to grow. They may attempt to make up to him or her for something the partner has missed in life. For example, one woman told me that she could sense when her husband needed the kind of love his

81

mother hadn't been able to give him. She intuitively understood his need for warm, affectionate "mothering," and was able to provide it without making him feel as if she was treating him like a child.

Similarly, a fifty-three-year-old man sensed that his lover had missed out on fatherly affection when she was a girl. They shared a full adult love, which included warm companionship, shared interests, and a rewarding sexual relationship. However, from time to time, he treated her in an affectionate, fatherly way, knowing it helped her feel cherished and feminine.

Sometimes lovers who know they are acting motherly or fatherly have doubts about whether that kind of love is real. At some level, they may feel that they are deceiving or manipulating their partners because they have understood the other person's deep psychological needs, and attempted to fulfill them. They may wonder whether they are loved in return simply because they fill these deeper needs. Or they might think that the relationship is only a substitute for a father-daughter or mother-son relationship.

This sort of relationship must be examined carefully before it is dismissed as fraudulent. The wish to fill the deepest needs of someone you love is usually a sign of caring and the desire to give. In addition, acting like a nurturing parent is typically just *one* aspect of the overall relationship. If the relationship works and no one is being hurt, why search for flaws? Romantic love is very complex and encompasses many levels of emotion.

On the other hand, some IP victims question whether they are worthy of someone else's love. As one woman said: "You can run into a big problem by presenting yourself as one person, when you know deep down you aren't really quite the way you present yourself. So you begin to feel fraudulent. In a romantic situation, no matter what a man says to compliment

82

you, if you really feel like shit, you say to yourself, 'Oh, he's just saying that because I'm wearing all this makeup, or because I bought this great dress. But he can't really see inside of me, or he would see how awful I really am.' "

These same feelings of fraudulence can be present when people move into the role of husband or wife. Spouses may feel uncomfortable with the expectations of their role, but play the role anyway. Or, they may meet those expectations only outwardly; inwardly, their feelings don't always match up with their behavior.

Some aspects of the husband and wife roles involve having to meet the outside world as "a couple." The wife of a high-ranking corporate executive, for example, may feel that she is not the perfect "corporate wife" she appears to be. She prepares elegant dinner parties for the company boss and his wife; she is gracious and charming at the corporate functions. Inside, though, she feels like the same small-town girl she was when she and her husband were first married. She fears that some faux pas will expose her as a fraud. Or she may know she plays the role to perfection, but be uncomfortable with it because it doesn't feel to her like "the real me."

Lois's second husband is a man who had already worked his way up to the presidency of a large firm in San Francisco. She is often called upon to assume the role of "the boss's wife." As she reported: "I put on a role for the outside world, especially in situations involving my husband's business. I am absolutely conscious of playing the role. Sometimes I even enjoy it; and sometimes I hate it. I decide how I should be and how I should appear. It's a very alien, odd way for me to be. I'm always afraid of these people, but I know they're afraid of me too, so I go out of my way to be nice and kind and businesslike and grown-up."

Twenty-five-year-old Christina grew up in the Midwest, and she spoke of her attempts to fit in with her boyfriend's conservative Southern family. She felt as if she was very different from them, and became quite aware of the disparity between the role she was playing and her internal feelings.

"When I first met his family and we went places together, I would just be in misery over clothes—over not having the right thing to wear," she said. "I would agonize over it. No matter what I chose, when I got there I would discover it was *not* the right thing.

"I always felt incredibly out of it with my boyfriend's family—out of my element. I never felt that I wasn't good enough, but that I just wasn't 'right.' I wasn't like them, and I couldn't fit in with them. They had values that were significantly different from mine. I couldn't be myself with them. I had to play a role."

Christina was caught in a conflict; she felt that she couldn't reveal her true self. Her motivations were sincere and well-intentioned. But in her efforts to please her boyfriend by trying to be like his family, she was feeling untrue to herself and to her own values. She felt like she was presenting a "false self."

I have treated couples in marital therapy who felt that they presented themselves to the community as ideal, loving couples. But they believed this image was phony because of some secret problem within the marriage. In one such case, the couple had been together almost thirty-five years and the marriage was basically a good one. When the two interacted in public—giving parties, attending social functions—their affection toward each other was real and sincere. People often commented on what an ideal, loving couple they were, and how much they seemed to enjoy each other. The fact that they didn't always act that way in private didn't mean they were presenting a false front. No two people can enjoy each other every minute.

Russell has been married for twenty-seven years and described his feelings this way: "Sometimes I feel fraudulent about being married a long time. There are times when you feel that you don't want to be married and that you're living a lie. You get caught up in it, and you feel like a fraud because you're doing the things you think you ought to do and maybe you don't really want to anymore."

However, Russell was able to see that he was making a rational choice to carry out his role as a husband during those times when he didn't really feel like it. It was a choice designed to protect and preserve the marital relationship in the long run. Few people feel like being married all the time. But do we abandon ship with our first feelings of inconstancy? Sometimes, in order to achieve a long-term goal, we have to do things we don't really feel like doing in the short run.

There are, of course, many other forms of love aside from romantic love. These types of feelings can also be subject to the Impostor Phenomenon. We can be afraid that those who love us will somehow discover that we are not who we appear to be, and this will cause us to lose their love.

Trudy has always had a close and loving relationship with her two nephews, who are now fourteen and sixteen years old. She and her husband regularly make the two-hour drive to visit them, always bringing gifts, and often taking them on outings. "I'm their 'exciting aunt.' I work in Hollywood and know lots of famous people. The boys and I have great fun together, and they think I'm this incredibly interesting, exotic woman who comes sweeping into town to see them," Trudy said. In her mind, she is not at all who they imagine her to be.

Last summer, Trudy's nephews came to stay with her for a week. Her husband was working out of town and it had been years since she had spent such an extended period of time alone with them. "I constantly felt that they weren't going to like me anymore after this," she said. "I thought they were going to find out what I was really like—a boring and awful person.

"The day my sister came to get them, one of them left without cleaning up the room he had been staying in. It was a complete mess. At first, I felt angry. Then, because I felt angry, I thought that he hated me, and not cleaning up was his secret way of telling me that I wasn't a special person to him."

THE IP AND THE PARENT

Another role that may elicit the feeling of being an impostor is that of parent. You can't really rehearse this role, because with every new stage in a child's development there's a whole world of new behavior to figure out. The feeling of being a fake can take over if you feel that you're not capable of handling this role well but must act as if you are, or if you feel that you are "posing" as a better parent than you actually are.

It is not unusual for a parent to question how good a job he is doing in raising his child, whether his decisions are always the right ones. This doesn't necessarily lead to believing that one is an impostor as a parent. If, however, a parent feels that his self-doubts must be kept secret to protect a false image he has created, he can begin to view himself as a fraud.

There are a number of reasons why parents doubt themselves, especially when their child is first born. When you have always been aware of being someone else's child, it can be hard to believe that you are now a "real" mother or father. For many years, when we see movies or plays or read novels, we identify with the characters who are the sons or daughters. We may have trouble suddenly identifying with the mothers and fathers.

Without really understanding it, a man may feel in some vague way that his own father is the "real" father; when he has a child, he is only pretending to be a father. A woman might have trouble reconciling the roles of daughter and mother in her self-image. The unfamiliarity of the new role, combined with the naturalness of the old one, can bring on a sense of pretense. But this should dissipate with time. We all need time to integrate the part of us that is still a son or a daughter with the role of parent.

Even during pregnancy, a woman faces questions that can lead her to wonder about her maternal instincts. Should she have natural childbirth and forego all pain-killing drugs? Is there something lacking in her if she opts for painless childbirth with anesthesia?

Once the baby arrives, she may feel hopelessly out of place at La Leche League meetings, but, like a "chameleon," she sits in silent agreement. Maybe she can't wait to stop breastfeeding (or chooses not to breastfeed at all). Then there are the times when the child's constant need for attention is driving her to distraction and all she wants to do is get out of the house. A woman with such feelings may begin to doubt her qualifications for motherhood and imagine that she must hide such "nonmaternal" instincts. Is she a "real" mother, she might wonder, or simply an impostor who lacks the natural gift for this calling? She's afraid that if she told anyone about her feelings, they would scornfully ask, "What kind of mother are you?"

Terry was an attractive young woman living with her husband and their three-year-old son in Florida. In secret, she worried endlessly because she had been told by a friend that she and her son had never "bonded." From the beginning, Terry had had doubts about herself as a mother. If her son cried while they were out on the street, she felt everyone was scrutinizing her, mentally criticizing her for being an inadequate mother. If she had to discipline him in public, she wondered if others would think her too cruel, or too lenient, if she did what came naturally. When she built sandcastles with him on the beach, she worried that others would see that she wasn't always enjoying it. Other mothers knew exactly what to do, she thought. She felt as if she were only acting as if she knew how to handle her child.

Despite her efforts to camouflage her feelings of inadequacy as a mother, Terry believed the only reason she actually appeared to be a real mother was simply because she had a child. She often felt like a child herself, and worried that the strangers who observed her with her son would discover that she wasn't a "real" mother after all.

Terry also believed that other mothers enjoyed staying at home with their children all the time, and only worked if they needed the money. She definitely did not enjoy being home with her son full-time, and became bored and irritated during the periods of time when this was necessary. She thought she was the only one who looked forward to going to work and who didn't mind leaving her child during the day.

Terry's image of what a "real" or "ideal" mother should be was far from realistic. Her instincts were usually correct, but she was so full of self-doubts in this role that she tried to do what she *thought* an ideal mother might do, rather than listening to those instincts.

Her discomfort with herself as a mother had its origins in Terry's past history. Her own mother had been physically ill for many years, and was quite depressed and emotionally unavailable to her. When Terry was just a small child, her mother ignored her a great deal, never reminding her to wash or helping her to get dressed for school. Terry hadn't had a good role model for motherhood, and this contributed to her later feelings of inadequacy and of being unable to identify herself as a "real" mother.

There are other pressures on parents that can also elicit feelings of fraudulence in this role. When divorced parents with children remarry, the readjustment in forming a stepfamily or merged family can cause emotions to run high all around.

Sean had two children from his first marriage, and when he remarried, it was to a woman with three children of her own. The children in this stepfamily fought bitterly with one another. Sean's oldest daughter was especially resentful toward her stepsisters. She felt they had a better room than she, got more clothes, and received all the attention. She refused even to eat at the same table with them.

Sean secretly felt that all this dissension was happening because he was an incompetent father. He didn't realize that his daughter was acting out her insecurities and fears about the new family situation. He was also confused about his role as stepfather. Should he discipline the stepchildren or leave that to their mother? He didn't know what to do and believed it was all his fault the children weren't getting along. The solutions he tried weren't working. He felt that he wasn't in control of the family—not "the head of the house," as he thought he should have been. Sean tried to act as if he knew what he was doing, but felt like a fraud as a father.

Sean had grown up without any role model for fathering; his father had been a weak and passive man who left Sean's mother when Sean was seven. So he developed his own standards based on an unrealistic ideal of what a father ought to be. He felt a "real" father should always be decisive, in charge, sure of himself. He wanted to live up to that image; because he could not, he saw himself as a complete failure.

With the growing number of dual-career families, even more questions can arise about what it means to be a "good" parent. Role confusion is everywhere. What is a father in today's society "supposed" to be doing? It's likely that his own father didn't change his diapers or cook strained beets for him, so he may see those activities as unmanly. But men are now being encouraged to share such jobs with their wives. A man might feel incompetent as a father because he doubts his ability to take care of an infant. Or he may feel guilty because he'd rather not get this involved in his child's daily routine. He can begin to think he is a fraud if he tries to hide these emotions, while constantly acting self-confident or enthusiastic.

The "superwoman"—wife-mother-executive who juggles all her responsibilities perfectly—is a common topic of conversation these days. If a woman tries to live up to the superwoman standard, she can wind up feeling that she's not doing a good job at any of these roles. This feeling may turn into the sense of being an impostor if she thinks she's fooling other people into believing that she is the ideal woman; secretly, she fears she's doing only a mediocre job at handling things, but wants to hide any signs of self-doubt.

An account executive at an advertising agency and the mother of two, Renata wants to be perfect both in her career and as a parent. Yet, with all her efforts, she said, "I feel like a double impostor. I'm not doing a good job anywhere. I feel like a fraud at work and a fraud at home. I don't read enough to keep up with my field because I'm too tired. And I don't enjoy spending time with my children at night because I'm too tired."

In fact, Renata spends an inordinate amount of time trying to be the perfect mother to her children. She seldom goes out at night and spends every weekend with her children. She takes an active role in the PTA, and is constantly carving out time to meet with teachers, chaperone class trips, and stay involved in school activities.

When Renata would like to go to bed early or have some time to herself after a hard day at work, she feels guilty. "Impostor" feelings arise because she knows that *others* observe her efforts at parenting and admire her for them. Other mothers often turn to her for advice about handling their own children. When she finds herself irritated or impatient with the children, she interprets this as inconsistent with the role of "the model mother." She sees it as evidence contradicting her public image. Her perfectionism leads her to think of herself as a secret failure and a fraud.

The desire to be absolutely perfect as a parent frequently has its roots in the image of one's own parents. It can come from one of two extremes. A woman who idealized her mother, or a man who worshipped his father, may feel that she or he can never equal that mythic, larger-than-life figure. One woman described her mother to me as being "beautiful, warm, talented, unselfish, one of a kind—impossible for me to live up to."

Perfectionism can also be based on trying to be everything that one's own parents were *not*. If our parents let us down somehow—or if we feel that they did—we may try to make up for their flaws by being perfect parents ourselves. The man who says, "I'll *never* yell at my children the way my father yelled at me" may cringe when he slips and loses his temper at them. A woman who swears she will *never* criticize her daughter the way her mother criticized her is horrified to hear herself blurt out to her three-year-old: "I *just* changed your clothes. Can't you ever stay clean for five minutes?"

We all say and do things we don't necessarily mean to, things we regret afterwards. But in the context of a parent-child relationship, such mistakes can be interpreted as failures to live up to an idealized picture of the perfect parent.

THE IP AND THE ADULT "CHILD"

An adult may feel that he is an impostor as a "devoted child" in dealing with his parents. Barring unusual circumstances, the role of a child in relation to his parents is very clear. We're supposed to love our parents and be grateful to them for giving us the gift of life. *Not* loving them is seen as abnormal. But, in truth, many people have mixed feelings toward their parents. They can love them but also feel angry and resentful about things that went on in the family's past.

A second aspect of the adult child's role toward his parents is that of duty. The grown child is expected to call home periodically, turn up at family gatherings, and take an interest in his parents' welfare. Should his parents become ill, he may have to assume responsibility for their care.

If an adult has mixed feelings towards his parents and his obligations to them, he can begin to feel that he is a phony as a "good" child. Feelings of fraudulence can develop if he feels he is deceiving others with his kind and generous expressions of love. Perhaps he calls his parents once a week to see how they are getting on and always acts cheerful on the phone. But, inside, he dreads these conversations and feels guilty about his "fraudulent" concern. He should *want* to talk to them, shouldn't he? Again, it is the feeling that being less than completely sincere at all times means that one has failed in his role, and is just a phony putting on a false front. Furthermore, he believes he must hide his "secret." Some people may experience guilt about having conflicting feelings toward their parents, but they feel a sense of relief after taking care of their filial duties. The person who thinks he is an impostor in this area feels worse: He believes he is only perpetrating a fraud.

Victor, a man in his late forties, had a good relationship with his mother. Even though he lived some distance away, he continued to visit her as she grew older, and then quite ill. "I loved her very much," he related, "but I felt fraudulent because I didn't put myself out for her. Not just when she got sick, but many times in her life when she needed my help. My brother lived near her and he had the total responsibility for her when she became ill.

"I used to say to my mother, 'Come and live with me.' But I always wondered to myself, 'Do I really want that?' And if she said yes, how would I have handled it? My life-style was so completely different from hers. I felt like a fraud, because a part of me really meant it, but I didn't know how I could handle it if it *really* came to fruition. I felt almost relieved that my brother lived nearby and was taking care of her, and I didn't have to take that responsibility. Well, it's true that he was closer, and I was about five hours away. But I feel very selfish about that. Sometimes you say or do things, and then you question yourself. You don't know if you're saying or doing something because it's the right thing to say, or you *should* do it. You feel like a fraud when you know you don't mean what you're saying one hundred percent."

Victor was experiencing conflicts and doubts about what he *would have done* in a situation that never came to pass. In this personal role, the situation would have been "the big one" for Victor—the one that had the potential to expose him as a fraud. Eventually, he saw that part of him wanted his mother to live with him, while another part did not. But he had been giving more weight to the part that did not. He was able to say, "Yes, I really did love my mother, but I didn't want to upset my life."

What Victor worried about was only a hypothetical situation, not a real one. He was guessing how he would have acted. In reality, his brother *was* more available to care for their mother. If circumstances had occurred to change that situation, Victor can't know for certain how he would have acted.

Many adults have had to face this type of situation as their parents age. Some may find emotions surfacing that they would much rather avoid.

When Lee's elderly mother broke her hip, she came to convalesce at her daughter's house for three months. Lee was beside herself with dread and guilt. "I hate having my mother near me, let alone in my house," she confided in me. "I can't stand it when she looks at me expectantly. She was always so mean to me when I was growing up, so critical. I really don't like her, but I feel like such a mean person. This is my *mother*. I'm her only child. She would never turn me away if the shoe was on the other foot. But all I can focus on is my own selfishness."

Lee was facing the stress of her fear of being exposed. She would have to "pretend" for three whole months to hide her negative feelings from her mother on a day-to-day basis. This situation could be her "big one." Her choice was to do this and feel fraudulent, or to hurt her mother deeply. If Lee hadn't actually been a concerned daughter, she would have done the latter.

THE IP AND SOCIAL SITUATIONS

Social situations can easily trigger "impostor" feelings. Those feelings can spring up when you are out at a party, meeting a group of new people. Maybe you're being charming, witty, and amusing. But inside you don't feel this way at all. That's when the questions start churning in your mind. Am I making a good impression? Do these people think I'm really boring or dumb?

Many people are insecure in social circumstances. If you feel that you are playing a part on the outside that doesn't reflect what "you really are," you can begin to feel like a fake. You're experiencing a sense of dissonance between the role you're playing and your internal feeling. And that dissonance tends to increase and reinforce the feeling of being a phony.

Possibly the most typical way in which people feel like social impostors is when they are shy, nervous, and self-conscious in social situations, and they attempt to hide their discomfort by trying to appear at ease.

Doug, twenty-nine, had been feeling like a "social impostor" since he was a teenager. When he was out with people his own age, he would shake inside and become fearful that he was literally shaking on the outside as well. This, he worried, would reveal to everyone that he was different, that he didn't fit in or belong—that he was a social failure. He himself tended to look down on other people in whom he detected signs of self-consciousness. He assumed others would regard him in the same way.

Even when he was with just one or two people, Doug felt it was important to be witty, talk a lot, and, in effect, be the center of attention. If he was performing well, then he would decide he was having a good time and feel good about himself. He viewed every social occasion as a performance event, and was obsessed with rating himself afterwards on how well he had done. If he had not "had a good time"—that is, hadn't performed well—he would become lethargic and depressed for days, thinking of himself as a failure.

Doug suffered from severe self-consciousness and thought all eyes were upon him in social situations. He felt tremendous pressure to hide his dreadful secret: that he was afraid he was "odd" and a social failure. So much of his energy was focused on performing well socially, he lost touch with his emotional sense of "having a good time." It was no longer a natural feeling, but something that was rated on a scale of objective criteria he had developed.

His feelings about the importance of social success and appearing to be at ease went back to Doug's past. His mother and brother were both socially extroverted and idealized by the family. His father, on the other hand, was withdrawn and ill at ease, not well-loved by the family members. He had a history of persistent psychological problems that had continually interfered in his social relationships. Doug feared that if he were introverted or shy, it would mean he was like his father, and he would be ostracized by others as his father had been.

In particular, hidden feelings of shyness can make one feel that he is only pretending to be something he's not. Some people are very successful at hiding shyness; to others, they appear to be quite extroverted.

In his book *Shyness,*[1] Dr. Philip Zimbardo, a social psychology professor at Stanford University, discusses the differences between the "publicly" and "privately" shy person. The publicly shy person is someone who can't hide his shyness and is highly uncomfortable about his feelings. The privately shy person, however, is capable of disguising his difficulties in social situations. People who are privately shy, Zimbardo notes, can often escape being detected, concealing their shyness with social skills they have learned well, or by staying away from situations in which they can't maintain control.

Zimbardo suggests that "shy people are often too concerned with whether or not their actions reflect their *real* selves." And this is the same feeling experienced by IP sufferers.

Feeling like a "social impostor" certainly doesn't mean that one can't lead a very active social life. Many people who see themselves as social impostors do exactly that. They simply make sure they keep secret their feelings about this aspect of themselves.

Nina, aged forty-four, frequently entertains in her home. Her efforts to appear perfect have been so successful, she has discovered that friends are reluctant to return her invitations because they feel they can't compete. "I so overdo it when we have friends over, they just don't feel that they can do the same," Nina explained. "Of course, I feel like if I don't do twice as much as everybody else, they'll discover I can do nothing at all.

"I try to keep in mind some of the realities, but it doesn't really keep me from behaving this way most of the time. I normally put forth two or three times the effort and energy most people would. It's not because I'm so wonderful, but because I'm a little bit crazy. I'm just afraid if I do less, they'll see that I'm totally incapable, that I can't even do a dinner party right."

Nina felt that she had to be the ideal hostess, to do better than anyone else, in order to mask her feelings of inadequacy.

THE IP AND APPEARANCE

For some IP victims, an attractive appearance is a very significant part of their public image. Usually, these individuals are naturally attractive and have been told so many times. Perhaps they have even accumulated evidence of their attractiveness as prom queens, winners of beauty contests, or photographers' models. Yet they believe their good looks are all artifice and facade—illusions they create to sustain their reputation as attractive people. They may feel naked and defenseless without elaborate hairstyles, makeup, and wardrobes. They are afraid that if they are seen without this "camouflage," they will be discovered as actually being ugly or simply ordinary looking. For some people, a pimple is cause enough to remain inside the house until they are once again "perfect."

Abby was a very naturally attractive woman in her late twenties. Although she was now of normal weight for her height, she could never get over her image of herself as a fat child. The memory of those years of overweight stuck with her, and she was unable to change her concept of herself. To disguise the overweight person she thought she was, she used elaborate makeup and wore very fashionable clothes. She had gotten into debt buying much more clothing than she needed. In fact, she had over forty-five pairs of shoes in her closet.

When Abby received compliments on her appearance, or was asked out on dates, she felt she had fooled others with all her cover-ups. She dreaded a relationship becoming intimate enough for anyone to see her without the clothes, shoes, and makeup. Then, she feared, she would be discovered as the fat, ugly girl she still felt herself to be.

Iris is in her early fifties and recalls her constant concern about her appearance during most of her life. A beautiful woman, she nonetheless felt that she had to put on a "mask" for the world. This required elaborate, time-consuming preparations. She interpreted these preparations as evidence that she was really a fraud.

As she explained: "For years, it took me three hours to get dressed every day. I didn't dare step out of the house without makeup because I thought I was so ugly. If every eyelash wasn't in place, or I didn't take pains with my hair, I just wasn't prepared to face the world, so I just wouldn't go out. I felt, 'This makeup is covering up the fraud who is me.' Without all this 'help' no one would care about me, or love me, or be attracted to me, or look at me.

"I always used to be late for social occasions. There was just never enough time to get myself together. Whenever I had to go somewhere, I would have to go out and buy a dress because I wasn't happy with what I had in my wardrobe. I needed that new dress to make me feel good. Maybe a lot of women don't carry it to the extreme I did, but I'm sure many women today need the props to present themselves to the world."

Iris's painstaking efforts with her appearance started when she was a teenager. The intent, though, wasn't to win people over. She said, "I just felt that I couldn't present myself to the world without the mask. I felt that if I didn't become this persona, I couldn't even step out of the house."

Over the years, Iris was able to understand and overcome her feelings of fraudulence and her anxieties about exposing herself to the world. In looking back, she attributes part of the problem to the standards of appearance that have traditionally been set for women in our culture, and to the marketing techniques that feed upon women's vulnerabilities in this area.

"I think that in our society, when you're being sold all these cosmetics, or going to the beauty shop, you're being set up in a way. If we have to go and have all this stuff done to us, then, when we don't have it on, we feel 'That is my social persona, and if I go out without it, people will find out what's underneath, and nobody will care about me.'

"Today, we have to get dressed up differently for everything we do. If we go to a discotheque, we have to get into our disco clothes; if we go into the business world, we have to wear our business clothes; if we go to the gym, we have to wear our gym clothes. If you don't conform, you're suspect. Most of us are so insecure, we can't risk not conforming to a very large degree. We wear the different clothes because underneath we feel fraudulent. Even as children—if you go to a Halloween party, you had better have a costume."

Some women displace their concerns about their appearance onto their homes. It then becomes critical to them that everything in the house be flawless before they invite anyone to come over. They also worry that someone may drop in unexpectedly when the house isn't looking perfect.

Feeling fraudulent about one's appearance doesn't necessarily have to be connected to the idea of beauty. A recent graduate may be used to thinking of himself as a person who wears sweatshirts and jeans, just as he did throughout his years in school. Suddenly, he is out in the working world, dressing in three-piece suits and carrying an attaché case. He must dress this way because it's appropriate to his new role. But it may take some time for him to stop regarding himself as a teenager playing "dress-up." He has to integrate the new role into his repertoire.

THE IP AND SOCIAL MOBILITY

Success can mean a dramatic change in life-style, and this may cause great confusion in a person's self-image. There is often far more involved than just having the money for a new house and car, lavish vacations, and new clothes. Success can also result in a change in one's social status group. Either financial success or recognition for accomplishments in one's field can bring about such a change.

This can be a particularly difficult adjustment to make for the person who comes from a working-class or poor background. Achievements or marriage into a higher socioeconomic level may propel this person into a new and unfamiliar world. IP victims who have this experience tend to feel thrust into a new social role that conflicts with the way they see themselves. It can take years for them to adjust to their new status; even decades later, some still wonder if they really "belong."

Virgil is sixty-seven, and talks about the discrepancy between his social origins and his present social status. "I come from very humble beginnings—a family of immigrants," he explained. "Now, I live in this fancy section of Beverly Hills, and the road from there to here is a long one. There are times when I'm not sure I really belong here. It would be very easy for me to feel like a fraud in some situations. It's like fulfilling a goal, a life's dream—to live in a house like this in a place like this was an incredible thing to be able to do for someone from my background. But at times, it brings out all my insecurities and I feel like a phony.

"Of course, when I really *think* about it, I realize that most of the people who live like this weren't born here! But when I'm feeling insecure, I have to ask myself, 'Do I really belong here?' My wife and I also belong to a very exclusive country club. Boy, if you want to really feel like a fraud! I think to myself, 'Do I really belong here? Well, of course I do, but at times I still question it—many times."

Over the years, Virgil has been able to put the emotional feeling of not belonging into perspective, and to see that it is an emotional sense of doubt, not a rational issue at all.

"I'm sure it isn't only me who feels this way," he reflected, "especially in American society, where people do get successful a lot—through a stroke of luck, or their own genius, or their hard labor. And I'm sure that when a lot of people get to that place, they have to ask: 'Do I really belong here?' They probably spend a lot of time on the psychoanalyst's couch."

THE IP AND THE "NICE PERSON"

In speaking with different people about their "impostor" feelings, another area seems to come up repeatedly that causes a great deal of emotional pain. This is being a "good" or "nice" person. People explain that although the world sees them as being basically nice or good, deep inside they often feel unworthy, mean, hostile, selfish, envious, and, sometimes, even evil. They believe that they have deceived others into liking or loving them by showing only nice or good feelings and behavior in public; they keep their "terrible" emotions and thoughts a shameful secret.

As one woman said, "It's always been hard for me to believe that somebody likes me or thinks well of me. I'm very well aware of all my evil, terrible thoughts. I'm always afraid that the world is going to discover them and find out that I'm not really a nice person, but that I'm really some horrible, cruel person."

People with these types of IP feelings assume, on an

emotional level, that thoughts are more "real" than actions. No matter how kind, charitable, or virtuous they act, if they have unkind, uncharitable, or less-than-virtuous thoughts, they interpret the contradiction by believing that the thoughts count more than the deeds.

April had grown up thinking of herself as someone who never got jealous. When she married a man who had a six-year-old daughter from his previous marriage, she was horrified to find herself resentful of the attention he bestowed on his child. He was devoted to the little girl and arranged to be with her as often as he could. April couldn't control her jealousy of the time, attention, and money he lavished on the child.

She kept her feelings secret, but April began to despise herself for what she called her "vicious" jealousy. How could she harbor such bitter feelings toward a mere child, she wondered. She felt like a phony whose sweet public image was hiding a "spoiled brat."

One reason for April's reaction to her feelings was the fact that she had been an only child. She had never had to cope with the competitive feelings that siblings often have to work out. These feelings burst upon her in adulthood, taking her by surprise when she was unprepared to deal with them.

This is how Anita, aged forty-four, described her feelings: "I feel I have to pay for anything I get. If somebody gives me something or does something for me, I'm immediately overwhelmed with the feeling that I have to make up for it. Because I'm not worthy, not the person they thought I was. If I was, I'd deserve it. But since I'm not, I don't. If someone gives me directions on the street, I feel like I have to run home and make them a pie."

Some IP victims have concerns that go beyond being "good human beings." They have a great preoccupation with the idea of being "nice." They can't bear the thought of ever being considered anything less than absolutely, totally nice all the time. This feeling can affect anyone, but I frequently hear it come from those people—particularly women—who have been known for their kind ways since childhood, and have much of their identity tied up with this role.

Typically, these individuals' public images of "niceness" have been based on a habit of never seeming to get angry. A child may become known as the sweetest, most gentle child in the family because he never outwardly expresses angry feelings. As he grows, he develops a habit of suppressing anger so he can maintain his image. He begins mistakenly to assume that truly nice people *don't* get angry. So he attempts to maintain a perfect record of "niceness."

This type of person is understanding, giving, sensitive, and empathic. He is a good listener, ready to provide his undivided attention to a friend's tale of woe at any time of the day or night. He will go to the ends of the earth to help his family, friends, boss, coworkers, even strangers.

It is crucial to him that other people always think of him as being nice. Never mind the raging snowstorm; he is happy to drive to the airport to pick up a friend's visiting aunt. You're preparing Thanksgiving dinner for twelve? She has her own family dinner to attend, but volunteers to help by picking up the flowers, the wine, and your dress at the cleaners. No favor is too large or too small to ask of this person.

Some of the accommodations this person makes extend beyond doing simple favors. Perhaps he is discussing what movie to see with a friend. In the end, it's likely they will wind up at the film the friend suggests. He doesn't want to appear to be a bad person by disagreeing or inflicting his opinion on his friend. It is far safer, he thinks, to sit through a movie he doesn't care about seeing than to risk making his friend unhappy.

When this pattern is carried over into the working world, it can have very serious consequences. The "nice person" may be well aware that he is being underpaid for that free-lance copywriting assignment, but can't bring himself to ask for more money or refuse the job. He winds up earning less than his talents deserve—which affects both his income and his image of himself as successful.

Meredith, a research analyst, described how she struggled with her image as a "nice" person in her work: "I'm a person who started out with very little feeling of a right to assert herself. You know—saying, 'I want, I need, don't do that.' If somebody said, 'Here's a dollar, go do ten dollars worth of work,' I would always do it. It wouldn't have occurred to me to say, 'Goddamnit, you have to pay me ten dollars.' I would have said, 'Yessir, and can I shine your boots?' I got way underpaid and way overworked, and never stuck up for myself in a business sense at all. It was my fault; it wasn't anybody else's."

Meredith recalls that her habit of being "nice" began in childhood. "It's a habit—a part of my personality," she related. "I took abuse from people and treated them reasonably. I sacrificed myself. Maybe it comes from the fear that one's anger is so strong, if you give vent to any of it, it will be disproportionate, as grotesque and cruel as it is in your imagination. As you begin to learn that anger is not unreasonable, and you are *not* cruel and horrible, you can express it more."

Other people may be completely unaware that they are imposing on this nice person with their requests. He's always seemed delighted to help them out. Frequently, he offers his services without being asked.

His friends and co-workers would think no less of him if he refused to do a favor, or weren't always first to volunteer for a job. But he can't believe this since he has built his reputation (he thinks) on his "niceness."

In reality, this individual typically *is* a nice person. But he is afraid that underneath the sweet exterior is a nasty, terrible individual with evil thoughts.

Over time, the stress of *always* being the good, helpful one with the sunny disposition builds up. The person feels obligated to accommodate others, no matter how inconvenient it is. The result is pent-up anger: anger at others for always expecting him to be there, anger at himself for always "going along." Those people who can recognize their anger are actually one step ahead; some can't bear to imagine that they might harbor such feelings at all. But rather than viewing their anger as a sign that something is wrong, they see it as confirmation of the fact that they are really not the nice people they "pretend" to be.

These feelings often surface in people who enter psychoanalysis. Psychoanalysis is a very intensive form of psychotherapy which involves reliving childhood emotions. During the process, people may rediscover childhood feelings and fantasies that they think are truly evil. Maybe they find that they had sexual feelings toward a parent; maybe at times they wished that their mother or father would go away forever. Such feelings are too powerful and frightening for a child to cope with. They must be repressed into the unconscious mind. In analysis, the repression may be lifted. Until they can forgive themselves for having had such feelings, while in analysis, people often go through a period of believing that they are hiding real malevolence underneath their public image.

THE IP AND THE GROWN-UP

Perhaps the one personal role I most often hear mentioned in connection to "impostor" feelings is that of the grown-up. As one woman said: "I'm impersonating a grown-up, but I'm really flunking adulthood."

Despite physical, social, and economic evidence to the contrary, many of us still feel like children inside. We want to believe that there is somebody "big" out there who will take care of us if things go wrong, or guide us along the correct path. It is sometimes difficult to believe that we are now the ones in charge; we must make the decisions and cope with crisis in the best way we can.

Along with being responsible for ourselves, many of us are responsible for the care of others. This realization can be a frightening one, and unconsciously we may wish to deny the reality of it.

That denial can be particularly difficult to maintain at certain times. One of those times is when we become a parent. It isn't always easy to reconcile this new role with the internal image of our childhood self, which we still feel very strongly inside.

When our own parents die, we step into their shoes, so to speak. We are forced to face the reality that they are no longer there to "take care of things," no matter how helpless and weak we feel. Even though we may actually have been living as very independent adults and rarely called upon our parents for help, this realization can still be a shattering one. It can bring our "helpless child" feelings into our consciousness.

I can remember instances of feeling like a helpless child when my own children were small—but I had to act like a grown-up so *they* wouldn't be frightened. These feelings came to me as brief flashes, but they were very unsettling. There was the car trip when we were hopelessly lost in the deep woods at night. Or the time when our dog was lost and I was afraid we would find him hit by a car, or never find him at all; how would I comfort my children then?

At times like those, I did my best to act like what I was supposed to be—the grown-up in charge—and to sound calm and reassuring. I didn't *feel* that I really knew what was best to do, but I knew that appearing this way was appropriate and necessary. Sometimes, we have to act "as if" because it's simply the right thing to do.

A letter I received from a successful corporate executive perfectly captured another side of feeling like an impostor as a grown-up. As he wrote: "I'm not a grown-up person, even though I am over forty-five years old and have teenaged children. It's difficult to impersonate a grown-up, but my profession and life-style involve a great deal of acting as an adult. I'm actually an adolescent, about fifteen, trapped in the life and body of a professional man, over forty-five, with kids, a house, et cetera.

"All of my success is due to a fairly good con I have worked up, consisting of the ability to pretend to be a normal grown-up person when that is necessary. And it is absolutely necessary for about fifty hours a week.

"If we go to a cocktail party, my wife knows that there is about a ninety-minute limit on my ability to talk with grown-ups and pretend to be one of them. Then, I have to excuse myself, and run off and eat popsicles, and play video games. . . . I can actually do what I have to in the way of my job and making cocktail party talk if need be; but I need to have R&R time to get over the strain of pretending to be a fairly normal professional adult.

"The funny thing is, I don't mind. I've never looked at it as a problem—just a given in life, as some of us are stuck with one problem and others have other problems. I suppose it is a bit anxiety-provoking. Pretending to be something you're not is always difficult, at least for me. But on the other hand, I believe I have more fun and enjoyment in life than many of my friends who are adults. I don't worry much about anyone exposing my fraud—I can fake it long enough to look good, I figure."

For people like this man, the feeling of being a fake as a grown-up is not that troubling. For others, it is more the feeling that one woman described this way: "I feel like I'm playing at being a grown-up, when what I really am is some frightened little kid."

There are two psychological concepts that are helpful in understanding how the Impostor Phenomenon finds its way into our lives. Although they also apply to the world of work, they show us how the IP can reach out to affect us in our personal roles. One is called the ego ideal. The other is the idea of a true self versus a false self.

THE EGO IDEAL

The term "ego ideal" was first used by Freud back in 1914.[2] Simply put, it is an internal standard by which a person measures himself and to which he aspires. The ego ideal is the image we feel we must live up to. Both consciously and unconsciously, we strive to achieve that image. We develop our ego ideal, or standard, early in life, by identifying with our parents and others who are significant figures to us.

People who are victims of the Impostor Phenomenon usually have very high and unrealistic ego ideals. When they see that they haven't met their own unattainable standards, they often feel guilty and ashamed. They expect the best from themselves, and nothing less. If they're not perfect, they think they must be failures. And they're afraid that others will find out that they are less than their own ideal of what they should be.

One woman reflected that her perfectionism in her work extended to her personal relationships with men. As she said: "I probably feel the same way there—that one will be rejected if one is less than perfect. I would never, ever expect somebody else to be perfect. But I would always expect it of myself."

The truth of the matter is that it is impossible to reach one's ego ideal. It is something we strive toward, but can never actually achieve. IP victims, however, blame themselves because they have fallen short of their goal.

When the person who feels like an impostor says, "I'm not a *real* friend, lover, parent, grown-up, et cetera," what he actually means is, "I'm not an *ideal* one." He is confusing the reality of his role with the perfectionistic standard of his ego ideal. He's measuring himself against something that *can't* exist. Yet he defines himself as a failure because he doesn't measure up.

The notion of the ego ideal is also very important when it comes to the career goals of high achievers who feel like fakes. To them, "less than perfect" equals failure, so praise and recognition are "mistakes" made by others, based on a fraud. They expect a flawless performance from themselves.

We all want to do well in our careers and we should certainly try to use our best efforts to accomplish this. The question is, at what point does the drive to excel turn into a compulsion to be perfect and a source of emotional pain? "I have to write the great American novel before I die, or I will die unhappy," said one man, a writer of forty. "It's the great American novel, or hara-kiri."

An attractive, straight-A college student, Veronica was also a talented artist, and active in local politics. She had come to therapy for one problem: bulimia. Ever since she had arrived at college, she had been deliberately vomiting after overeating at meals. Although she had struggled with a weight problem for most of her life, she was always able to take off any extra weight she gained. At school, she reverted to vomiting as a quick solution.

Veronica said she was depressed only about her weight problem. But after several sessions, she reported that she was finding it difficult to study. When particularly frustrated and anxious, she had crying spells. "I get hyper and paranoid," she said. She was afraid that she wouldn't be able to pull her work together in time for her deadlines.

At this time, she was feeling especially anxious because she needed to ask her advisor—whom she scarcely knew—for a recommendation to business school. When asked what frightened her, she replied at first: "He's a misogynist." Then: "I'm afraid that when I go to talk to him, he'll find out I'm not really bright. Now he only sees my grades, which look pretty good, but when he finds out I don't really know enough, he won't want to give me the recommendation."

Veronica contrasted herself with her husband, also in school, who had no hesitation about asking for recommendations. He was less disciplined about studying, she said, and had a lower average; but he was "self-confident, open, and gregarious" in class and with professors. Veronica interpreted this as evidence that her husband was truly bright and had nothing to hide, whereas she was a mere impostor, whose hard-earned grades masked her intellectual deficiency.

As therapy continued, Veronica learned that her

self-imposed perfectionistic demands on herself were beyond anyone's capacity to fulfill. They extended to all areas of her life: studies, art, relationships, appearance, and weight. She needed to resort to a shortcut somewhere, so she controlled her weight by vomiting.

Mona's mother had been living vicariously through her daughter for many years, taking charge and instructing Mona on what kinds of work she should take on. Because she was very bright, Mona had been able to pursue the studies and jobs that her mother considered to be worthy and of high status. But after she had some success with one thing, Mona would immediately switch to another field. Finally, in order to feel that she was truly on her own, she left her home in Houston and moved East.

Around the time Mona reached her early thirties, she found herself waking up in the middle of the night with feelings of panic and shame. She would think, "I must be a terrible person. I committed myself to those things and I haven't cared about them since. I must have no sense of commitment, no ideals at all." Usually, these late-night episodes occurred when Mona was about to be interviewed for a job she had chosen herself. She worried that the interviewer would see all those changes on her résumé and discover her dreadful secret.

Eventually, Mona was able to see that she hadn't let down her own ideals. In fact, she'd never had a chance to develop any of her own. Without knowing it, she'd been trying to live up to her mother's strict and overinflated ego ideal. She had adopted her mother's "voice" as her own, and it was that voice that was punishing her during the night.

THE TRUE SELF VERSUS THE FALSE SELF

What is the "self"? Psychologists, sociologists, philosophers, and just about everybody else have been debating this for centuries. But most of us instinctively understand that we have our private side and our public side. Which one of these is the "true self"—or whether both can be "true"—has never been agreed upon.

Here are some of the ways that psychologists have attempted to explain the idea of the self:

Social psychologist Leon Festinger feels that all people strive for consistency and congruity.[3] According to Festinger, people experience internal conflict when they observe themselves behaving publicly in a way that is dissonant or inconsistent with their private self-image.

Others, however, don't go along with Festinger's thinking. In fact, some psychologists believe that the self is actually multiple in nature. They see it as flexible enough to tolerate inconsistencies *without* experiencing conflict.

As early as 1890, psychologist William James differentiated the inner/subjective self from the social self.[4] He said that a person has as many social selves as there are individuals who carry an image of that person in their minds.

Sociologist Erving Goffman describes all social relationships as requiring "facework."[5] He proposes that it's normal and natural to behave differently in different roles as a way of adapting to various situations. He views all social interactions as being like theatrical performances in which each person acts out a "line" calculated to achieve some ultimate payoff. The self, then, is simply a performance designed to impress or win over other people.

113

Kenneth Gergen, a social psychologist, also rejects the notion that people strive to have a singular and consistent self-image.[6] He feels that when people perceive that they present themselves differently in different situations, they don't normally see this as discrepant with their identities. Instead, they change or expand their identities to accommodate all their self-presentations.

Still another way of looking at it is offered by Mark Snyder, a professor of psychology at the University of Minnesota. He suggests that it is perfectly normal to be *either* singular and consistent, or to be multidimensional. In his view, it depends on a trait he calls "self-monitoring."[7] Self-monitoring has to do with how much a person engages in "impression management," meaning the extent to which he tries to control the impressions and images that other people form of him in social circumstances.

According to Snyder, low self-monitors appear to lack the ability, talent, or desire to vary their self-presentation. They act in a consistent fashion from one situation to the next. He says that they value the idea that "what they do" should reflect "who they are." They appear oblivious to the role or image that might be most desirable for them to adopt in a particular situation. Instead, they seek to exhibit a "me for all times"—a "principled self," a person with one consistent identity.

This doesn't mean that low self-monitors act inappropriately in situations. But they resist compromise and strive to express what they feel internally. This is their approach to interpersonal relationships, and it is the one with which they feel most comfortable. Low self-monitors abide by the words of Shakespeare: "This above all—to thine own self be true. And it must follow, as the night the day, thou canst not then be false to any man."

In contrast, high self-monitors possess a versatile repertoire of "impression management" skills. In any given situation, they are naturally attuned to picking up cues about desirable roles and images. They strive to portray, says Snyder, "the right person in the right place at the right time."

Snyder views high self-monitors as having a "pragmatic self," capable of acknowledging multiple and contradictory roles which fit many different situations. He feels that high self-monitors reflect Erving Goffman's view that life is theater and the self is simply the sum of one's different performances.

Psychologist and professor Edward Sampson of Clark University has also written about the self-monitor.[8] Sampson found that high self-monitors define their identities in terms of external features, such as their occupations or memberships in various groups. Low self-monitors, he notes, define their identities more in terms of internal features, such as feelings, motives, and personality characteristics.

Interestingly, one study has shown that high self-monitors are so adept themselves at impression management, they are particularly alert to the impression-management strategies of others. In a 1976 study of high and low self-monitors, researchers simulated the television game show "To Tell the Truth."[9] They showed that high self-monitors were better than low self-monitors at unmasking the confederates. The results suggested that high self-monitors should be less easily deceived than low self-monitors by flattery or other impression-management strategies practiced by other people.

A high self-monitor may see himself in a positive way: as a multidimensional, flexible individual with many aspects to his identity. But an IP victim who also uses impression management well tends to interpret it as false, inconsistent, manipulative, phony—more evidence that he is a mere impostor. He regards impression management more as a vice than a virtue. It is as if these skills were tinged with immorality instead of simply being useful talents for social adjustment, and sometimes a necessary part of a successful career. The ability to self-monitor is not a vice. In fact, Snyder has conducted research showing that it is separate and distinct from such things as lying, Machiavellianism, and psychopathic deviance.

The many roles that each individual plays may be seen simply as different dimensions of one self. If they weren't all part of us, we wouldn't be capable of playing them. When someone says, "I'm not myself today" (usually to excuse anger, irritability, or odd behavior), he is being misleading. Of course he is himself; who else could he possibly be? What he is really grappling with is a part of himself that is either unfamiliar to him, or is one he might like to disown or deny. But the behavior he is exhibiting is still one part of his true, or whole, self.

People who suffer from the Impostor Phenomenon make the assumption that there is only one "true self," and that it should be singular and consistent, never varying from one situation to another. When they see inconsistencies between their inner feelings and their outer behavior, they tend to equate the public image with falseness and the private image with truth. They show that they have many "selves," but assume that only one can be "the real me." The others, by default, must be false selves.

If you believe that you are presenting a false self to the world, you have made a case to yourself that you are a fraud. When the "good friend," "good parent," or "good child" sees his behavior as conflicting with the inner self, he assumes that he is being phony on the outside—and that he is fooling others into thinking he's something that he is not.

116

Sometimes, people are confused about which aspect of their personalities is "the real me" and which is "the impostor." They may begin to wonder if they actually have a "split personality." (I've especially noticed this question come up among patients just after *Sybil* or *The Three Faces of Eve* has been shown on television.) What is usually happening is that these people are having trouble accepting and integrating different emotions and traits into their self-images. They are having difficulty seeing themselves as whole people with more than one dimension.

In some instances, a person might feel that by re-orchestrating his self-presentation to fit various roles, he is *destroying* the inner, or private, self. The late actor Peter Sellers claimed that he had no private self or personality outside his creations. Said Sellers: "There used to be a real me, but I had it surgically removed."[10] One critic speculated that, in being all things to all people, Sellers became nothing to himself; that his relentless compulsion to work represented a search for the character that was, in reality, the misplaced Peter Sellers.[11]

We also learn that discrepancies exist between the public and private selves through our dealings with other people. In everyday life, we seldom take people at face value, assuming that there is more to a person than meets the eye.

In his novel *Being There*, Jerzy Kosinski offered a twist on this idea in the character of Chance, the gardener. Until circumstances forced him out of his home, Chance knew nothing of the world except what he had learned from watching television and attending to his garden. The other people who came into contact with him strained to interpret his simpleminded pronouncements as profound. By failing to take his words at face value, they didn't recognize that there was actually *less* to Chance than met the eye. These other characters assumed that there was a discrepancy between his simple public self and some deeper private reality. (You might remember that, interestingly enough, it was Peter Sellers who played the part of Chance in the film version of this novel.)

The late psychoanalyst Donald Winnicott is widely known for his theory of the false self.[12] He explained that the fear of having one's true self discovered is related to the feeling that there is something shameful about it. The individual regards it as incompetent, weak, or needy in some way. In his view, the "false" or compliant self protects the true self.

An IP victim may also see his public self as a sort of disguise that protects the "true" self from exposure. This public, or "false," self meets what he *feels* are other people's expectations. He is afraid that "if only they knew the *real* me, I would lose what's important (their love, respect, admiration, acceptance, etc.)." The true self, he feels, with its privately perceived imperfections and flaws, must be hidden. This leads to the feeling that he is manipulating or fooling others with a false public image. As a result, he feels that he doesn't deserve whatever positive feedback he receives from other people. In his mind, that praise is based on a partial, rather than a whole, truth.

Psychologist Norma K. Lawler looked into the connection between "impostor" feelings and this notion of layers of the self in a study she conducted in 1984.[13] As part of her research, Lawler gave the Harvey IP Scale to 130 college and graduate students. She then interpreted their drawings of concentric circles, which symbolized the layers of their "selves." She compared their scores on the IP Scale with the circles they had drawn.

Those students who scored highest on the IP Scale had a significant difference between the sizes of their inner and outer circles compared to students with lower scores on the Scale. Lawler concluded that these high-scoring students tended to emphasize the level or part of themselves that they most often presented to the world; they de-emphasized the level or part of themselves that they shielded from the world.

Dr. Howard Huxster, a psychiatrist at the Institute of Pennsylvania Hospital and a psychoanalyst for twenty years, related to me that *every* patient he has treated through analysis has experienced the sense of being an impostor. Observes Dr. Huxster: "After getting deep into psychoanalysis, every single patient becomes acutely aware that each person lives in his or her own private world of feelings, experiences, and behaviors, and there is no way to communicate this to others in its entirety. So nobody is exactly what he seems to be."

Most people who suffer from the IP in their personal roles are perfectionists and fear the loss of love if they should be "discovered" as ordinary, average human beings. They believe that others require them to be ideal, flawless in their roles. But this usually turns out to be an internal requirement, one they have set for themselves. They fear that they are accepted *only* for their "specialness," and that if they are revealed as average—not better than others—they will lose that sense of uniqueness and the acceptance that goes with it.

Other IP victims feel fraudulent because they haven't yet integrated one or more of their new roles into a unified sense of self. New roles we take on and new emotions we discover within ourselves may feel alien at first, leading to conflicting views of ourselves. This can cause us to wonder, "Who is the real me?" Yet, as we grow better acquainted with our various "selves" and more experienced with our new roles, we should come to see them as different dimensions of one whole person.

Do You Believe
You're an Impostor?

FOUR

The Impostor Phenomenon is not easily revealed, nor easily recognizable. By its very nature, it is a secret experience. I designed the Harvey IP Scale to help psychologists identify these feelings in the course of their research and compare their findings. The Scale and the additional questions in this chapter can also help you to explore your own IP issues. They will enable you to get in touch with any "impostor" feelings you might have.

Bear in mind that these questions are not designed to provide a definitive diagnosis. They can't take the place of a qualified therapist. They are only meant to act as tools to help you discover your feelings. And, remember, there are degrees of the "impostor" experience: It ranges all the way from mild to severe. But by examining certain feelings, you can consider if, and how, the IP may be affecting your life.

Find a comfortable, quiet spot for yourself before you start to answer these questions. Take some time to reflect on areas of your life that may cause you anxiety and give rise to a feeling that you are not "what you appear to be." Think about what you are doing when you feel this anxiety. If you can tie in your feelings of fraudulence with the specific role (or roles) you are

123

playing when they occur, you'll be taking an important first step toward understanding how the Impostor Phenomenon might be influencing you.

The questions are divided into two sections. Most of the questions in Part I relate to roles in work and academic study. Start by going through all of them once, focusing on your job or school program. Then, go back and re-read the questions, keeping in mind some other roles you play. You might think about your role as friend, parent, lover, spouse, or simply "grown-up." Some people's IP feelings are related to very specific aspects of their personal lives and emotions. Among the most commonly mentioned areas are appearance, socializing, loyalty, altruism, and love. Not every question in Part I will apply to personal roles, but it is helpful to jot down notes on those that do.

After you have completed Part I, you will see how to add up your score. What follows is an explanation of all the questions, showing how each one relates to some aspect of the Impostor Phenomenon.

In Part II, you can look more closely at how the IP may be influencing you in your work and in your personal life. These questions are open-ended: You can answer them in any way you choose and at any length. They are here for your private reflections, to help you form a picture of why you feel like an impostor, how you react to this feeling in your everyday life, and why you have come to feel this way.

PART I

For each item below, place a check mark in the box that best indicates how true of you the statement is. Your first thoughts and impressions are most important here, so answer as quickly and honestly as possible.

1. In general, people tend to believe I am more competent than I really am.
NOT AT ALL TRUE   VERY TRUE
A ☐ B ☐ C ☐ D ☐ E ☐ F ☐ G ☐

2. I am certain my present level of achievement results from true ability.
NOT AT ALL TRUE   VERY TRUE
A ☐ B ☐ C ☐ D ☐ E ☐ F ☐ G ☐

3. Sometimes I am afraid I will be discovered for who I really am.
NOT AT ALL TRUE   VERY TRUE
A ☐ B ☐ C ☐ D ☐ E ☐ F ☐ G ☐

4. I find it easy to accept compliments about my competence.
NOT AT ALL TRUE   VERY TRUE
A ☐ B ☐ C ☐ D ☐ E ☐ F ☐ G ☐

5. I feel I deserve whatever honors, recognition, or praise I receive.
NOT AT ALL TRUE   VERY TRUE
A ☐ B ☐ C ☐ D ☐ E ☐ F ☐ G ☐

6. At times, I have felt I am in my present position or academic program through some kind of mistake.
NOT AT ALL TRUE   VERY TRUE
A ☐ B ☐ C ☐ D ☐ E ☐ F ☐ G ☐

7. I feel confident that I will succeed in the future.
NOT AT ALL TRUE   VERY TRUE
A ☐ B ☐ C ☐ D ☐ E ☐ F ☐ G ☐

8. I tend to feel like a phony.
NOT AT ALL TRUE   VERY TRUE
A ☐ B ☐ C ☐ D ☐ E ☐ F ☐ G ☐

9. My personality or charm often makes a strong impression on people in authority.
NOT AT ALL TRUE   VERY TRUE
A ☐   B ☐   C ☐   D ☐   E ☐   F ☐   G ☐

10. I consider my accomplishments adequate for this stage in my life.
NOT AT ALL TRUE   VERY TRUE
A ☐   B ☐   C ☐   D ☐   E ☐   F ☐   G ☐

11. In discussions, if I disagree with my boss, a professor, or the person in charge, I speak out.
NOT AT ALL TRUE   VERY TRUE
A ☐   B ☐   C ☐   D ☐   E ☐   F ☐   G ☐

12. I often achieve success on a project, report, or test when I have anticipated I would fail.
NOT AT ALL TRUE   VERY TRUE
A ☐   B ☐   C ☐   D ☐   E ☐   F ☐   G ☐

13. I often feel I am concealing secrets about myself from others.
NOT AT ALL TRUE   VERY TRUE
A ☐   B ☐   C ☐   D ☐   E ☐   F ☐   G ☐

14. My public and private self are the same person.
NOT AT ALL TRUE   VERY TRUE
A ☐   B ☐   C ☐   D ☐   E ☐   F ☐   G ☐

SCORING

For each question, match the number of points to the letter beside your check mark. For example: In statement #1, (G) = 6, so a check mark next to the letter (G) equals 6 points. Add 6 points for this question to your total score.

Statement

1	A=0	B=1	C=2	D=3	E=4	F=5	G=6
2	A=6	B=5	C=4	D=3	E=2	F=1	G=0
3	A=0	B=1	C=2	D=3	E=4	F=5	G=6
4	A=6	B=5	C=4	D=3	E=2	F=1	G=0
5	A=6	B=5	C=4	D=3	E=2	F=1	G=0
6	A=0	B=1	C=2	D=3	E=4	F=5	G=6
7	A=6	B=5	C=4	D=3	E=2	F=1	G=0
8	A=0	B=1	C=2	D=3	E=4	F=5	G=6
9	A=0	B=1	C=2	D=3	E=4	F=5	G=6
10	A=6	B=5	C=4	D=3	E=2	F=1	G=0
11	A=6	B=5	C=4	D=3	E=2	F=1	G=0
12	A=0	B=1	C=2	D=3	E=4	F=5	G=6
13	A=0	B=1	C=2	D=3	E=4	F=5	G=6
14	A=6	B=5	C=4	D=3	E=2	F=1	G=0

These fourteen statements make up the Harvey IP Scale. This scale is designed to measure the Impostor Phenomenon in an individual. There is no one score that means "Yes, you have the IP" or "No, you don't have the IP." The scale measures how weak or how strong one's "impostor" feelings may be. A score leaning toward the high end suggests that you experience strong IP feelings. A low score suggests mild or minimal symptoms of the IP. The highest possible score is 84; the lowest is zero.

Now that you have added up your own score, you can get some idea of whether the Impostor Phenomenon might be affecting your life. Perhaps you had a relatively low score, indicating that you may have a mild case of the IP. If your score was in the middle range (in the vicinity of 42 points), you may be more troubled by "impostor" feelings. If your score was in the upper range, the IP is likely to be causing you significant anxiety and quite possibly preventing you from accomplishing all that you might.

DISCUSSION OF PART I

Statement #1. "In general, people tend to believe I am more competent than I really am."

Competence is frequently a major issue for victims of the Impostor Phenomenon. If you checked off "Very True" and had a high score on this question, then you know that other people *do* see you as competent. Yet you believe that they have overestimated you in some way.

This is how a social worker described his feelings about his own competence: "Sometimes, the impostor feelings come out when I'm teaching or supervising other people in training. I feel on the spot as a supervisor—like they're going to find out I really don't know any more than they do. People have told me I act authoritative, and as if I know exactly what I'm doing in research and other areas. But what they see as me is what I see as my cover-up. I act that way so that people won't challenge me—like they wouldn't dare. Because if they did, they might find out I don't know enough."

When we think of a competent person, we envision someone who has the ability to get things done. You may always accomplish what you set out to do, but if you feel that you are an impostor, you probably assume your achievements aren't due to your competence. Instead, you might think that you're simply good with people, a smooth talker on the telephone, just lucky, etc.—whatever it is you think is helping you "get by."

IP victims often believe that they are competent in *certain* areas, but not in the areas that they see as the *real* measure of intelligence and ability. Some artists, for example, believe they have technical competence, but lack originality. A writer told me he believed for a long time that he couldn't possibly be good at what he does because he misspelled so many words.

Think about what the word "competence" means to you. What does it imply in terms of your job? What does it mean to be a competent parent? What does it take to be considered competent in these roles? Think of someone who performs the same role that you do whom you consider to be competent. What does that person do that's different from what you do? What are the areas in which you *do* feel competent?

Statement #2. "I am certain that my present level of achievement results from true ability."

If you answered this question "Very true," then you believe in the validity of your accomplishments. People who believe they are frauds do not. If you checked an answer somewhere in the middle, you may experience some doubt in this area. An answer of "Not at all true" suggests very strong IP feelings.

Victims of the Impostor Phenomenon minimize the importance of true ability in their success. In Chapter 1, we saw how they provide explanations for their achievements that have little or nothing to do with ability.

Psychologist Harold Kelley proposed a principle that helps to explain why IP victims don't attribute their successes to talent and ability. I mentioned one of Kelley's principles in Chapter 2; he was the one who talked about covariation, and experimenting like scientists with cause and effect in our lives. He calls the second principle "discounting."[1]

The principle of discounting states that if a person can perceive more than one cause for an event, he tends to discount a single cause in proportion to the number of alternative causes. In other words, the greater the number of possible causes, the less weight an individual will give to one particular cause.

IP victims perceive any number of possible causes for their accomplishments—hard work, personality, good timing. But they may grant less importance than they should to their natural abilities and talents. They often have several outstanding assets, such as good looks, sensitivity, and charm, and this makes matters even more confusing. They begin to believe that true ability plays only a very small part in the cause-and-effect relationship of success.

Below are some typical examples of the ways that IP victims explain their success. After each statement, I have noted the factor to which this person is actually attributing his accomplishments. Notice how the word *just* acts to discount any "real" ability:

"I was just very fortunate . . . I just happened to be in the right place at the right time." (LUCK)

"I'm just an overachiever . . . I work twice as hard and twice as long as anybody else . . . I just have a lot of perseverance. I outlast the competition by hanging in there the longest." (EFFORT)

"I just know how to get along with people . . . I'm extroverted, and I have a good sense of humor, so I relate well to people and make a good impression . . . People like me." (SOCIAL SKILLS)

"I just figure out what people want and give it to them . . . I have a good sense of what people are looking for, and I can present myself as exactly that." (INTUITION AND SENSITIVITY)

"I just happened to be born into the right family . . .

I had the right connections." (UNFAIR ADVANTAGES)

Although these other causes do play some part in high achievement—and that's especially true for hard work—it takes genuine ability to produce ongoing success. This is a critical point, which anyone who feels like a fake must remember. *Ability is more reliable than any other cause of success*. It is a relatively permanent and enduring quality that sustains success. Simply put, it is a *necessary* component in reaching high levels of achievement.

Statement #3. "Sometimes I am afraid I will be discovered for who I really am."

If you answered this question in the direction of "Very true," you experience the IP victim's conflict over his public and private images. And you know the fear of exposure as well.

IP sufferers tend to view the private self as the "true self" and the public self as the "false self." They talk about the person "I *really* am," referring to a private self, which is hidden from and cannot be known by others.

High scorers on this statement tend to interpret any discrepancy between their public and private selves as evidence that one is true and one is false. In reality, both selves may be perfectly valid—but they simply aren't integrated with each other in the person's mind.

In the comments below, you can see how IP victims typically express the sense of a public self "hiding" a secret and shameful private self:

"People think I'm very bright and a good conversationalist, but I'm really just a dilettante. I know a little about a lot of things, so they think I'm smarter than I am. If they looked for depth, they would find out how shallow my knowledge really is."

"Although I appear to be a grown-up, I'm really just

a child inside. My children think I know what I'm doing, but I'm really scared to death."

"Men think I'm very beautiful and compliment me all the time. But they don't see me without all the makeup and my hair not fixed. Without makeup, I'd be nothing—they wouldn't look at me twice."

"I act like I'm very self-confident. Everything is 'No problem.' People can't see that inside, I'm quaking in my boots."

Statement #4. "I find it easy to accept compliments."

The Shrinking Violet would have to disagree with this statement. If you found this statement to be "Not at all true" of yourself, you may fit into this pattern. Think about why you find it difficult to accept praise or expressions of admiration. Are you afraid of appearing arrogant? Do you feel you will be setting yourself up for a fall, should people find out that your work isn't as good as they had originally thought?

Take a look at some typical examples of Shrinking Violet responses to praise. Do you recognize your own words in any of them?

Comment: "You're very intelligent and perceptive."
Response: "Oh, I just have a flair for expressing things. I'm good with words."

Comment: "You're a great cook. You sure know how to prepare a wonderful dinner."
Response: "Well, I use a lot of mixes and just throw in a few extra ingredients. And I got the dessert already prepared from the gourmet shop down the street."

Comment: "You gave a terrific presentation at the meeting this morning."

Response: "Yes, but did you notice how uncertain I was on the final figures? It's a good thing the client didn't. I really bluffed my way through it."

Comment: "I saw a copy of that report you wrote. Nice job."

Response: "Thank goodness Research lent me that crackerjack new assistant for a few days. I could never have pulled it all together in time without her."

IP victims often disown praise and discount the expertise of the people who offer it. They begin to view those who have complimented them as blind to the truth, too dumb to know any better, "seduced" by their "tricks."

They may not accept that the praise really relates to *them* as individuals. As an executive commented: "People have a need to believe that someone can put things together and know what he's doing. They just see what they want to see in me." Or else they may be suspicious of compliments, believing that the other person is using flattery to get something from them. One woman interpreted praise from her boss in this way: "He's just telling me my work is good in order to dump a lot of extra projects on me."

Statement #5. "I feel I deserve whatever honors, recognition, or praise I receive."

The high IP score on this statement leans toward the "Not at all true" response. If you believe that you are an impostor, then you are likely to feel that any success or public recognition of success must be undeserved.

Take the example of a highly accomplished literature professor. Throughout his career, this man had continually received awards, fellowships, and promotions;

he was elected to the top office of any group he joined. Yet whenever people commented on how well he was doing, he would respond by saying: "Life continues to treat me better than I deserve."

Seth is now in his late fifties, with a highly successful career as a scriptwriter for television. He feels that he is only playing at being a grown-up in his work. As one example of his "impostor" feelings, he describes how he felt when he had to address a large group at an important meeting. "I thought, 'I don't know anything, they're all grown-up people, they're all making money,' " he remembered. "And I'd get up and be funny and nice and warm. Everyone would applaud; they'd love what I said and I would feel okay. But then I would feel that I didn't belong there doing that."

At the same time, Seth knows that he is good at his work. Yet he feels that he doesn't deserve to make as much money as he does for it. Earlier in his career, he commented, "In a very short time, I was making tons of money—but I was disturbed by it. I actually saw a therapist half a dozen times. I was troubled about making so much money because I didn't deserve it; it was easy for me to do." Even today, he says, "I give away a lot of money. You name it, people get money from me. I'm really an easy touch, because I don't feel I should have it. It's like 'What did you do to earn it?' "

Even though he is aware of how skilled he is in his profession, Seth had never planned to do this type of writing. "I sort of fell into this as a way of making a good living," he explained. "My problem is I never learned to put a value on it. Here's a kid who always knew he was going to grow up to be a novelist. I still feel that that kid was not realized."

IP victims may take the idea of undeserved recognition one step further. For several days, one man persisted in believing that his unexpected promotion at work was not real; he felt his name had been added to the list of promotions purely by error.

Statement #6. "At times I have felt I am in my present position or program through some kind of mistake."

An answer leaning in the direction of "Very true" suggests another IP symptom. IP victims sometimes question the basis for their being in a particular situation in the first place. The phrase "at times" is important here. An IP victim isn't necessarily *certain* that a mistake has been made. Instead, it may be a sense of doubt that is contributing to his "impostor" feelings. At times, he does feel qualified—but at other times he's not at all sure. He may *intellectually* acknowledge that he is qualified or trained to do the job, but *emotionally* he feels otherwise.

To "know" something intellectually and to "know" something emotionally are two different experiences for many people. There is often inconsistency between the two types of "knowing." For the IP victim, this can lead to self-doubt. The Impostor Phenomenon is more of an emotional, or "feeling," kind of knowledge than an intellectual one. If you feel like an impostor, you may waver back and forth in a state of uncertainty about whether you truly belong at your present level of achievement in your job or in some other personal role you play.

You might have achieved a great deal in a field for which you are qualified, but don't really like. Some IP victims never made a free or conscious choice of career. One way this happens is if they were psychologically programmed to fulfill the wishes of their parents.

For example, one woman described how she went to work at her father's company because it would fulfill her father's dream and compensate for her brother's failure to fulfill *his* potential. Yet she secretly wanted

135

to study acting, and found the daily schedule and style of an executive's life entirely incompatible with the way she wanted to live. Although she did well in the business, she never felt like her achievements were her own.

Sometimes an individual believes he should pursue a certain career or personal role because it's the "right" thing to do. One man in his fifties told me how he had become a lawyer because that was *the* prestigious, money-making career for his generation, and he had both the ability and the grades. He eventually realized that it felt false to him and switched to a different field.

We don't know how many women in past generations had secret longings to pursue a career, but believed that the "right" thing to do was to stay home with the children. Today we might find the reverse situation: Some women might prefer to raise their children full-time and not go to work. But many now feel that a woman *should* work, that there's something shameful about being "just a mother and housewife."

An IP victim's anxiety is increased by feeling that some mistake may have been made or that he has fallen into his present position by a random twist of fate. He fears that his success is an illusion, which may vanish at any time, rather than a valid achievement, based upon reality, which will endure. And the idea that fate or luck is at work here leaves him with little sense of control over what might happen. The feeling that one is not in control can also provoke great anxiety.

Statement #7. "I feel confident that I will succeed in the future."

In order to have confidence in our continued success, we must believe we have an enduring, permanent quality that can be called upon again and again. A victim of the Impostor Phenomenon tends to feel that something is missing in him which is necessary for continued success.

If someone in a creative field secretly believes he lacks real creativity or originality, he may fear he can't sustain his reputation because he can't rely on that quality in the future. A writer explained his feelings about creativity this way:

"The problem with creative leaps is that they are flashes of inspiration. They don't come with consistency. I hope something will present itself as I read and think and talk to people. When it does, I feel 'Oh boy, thank goodness—I got it' and I feel very pleased. But there's no sense it's going to happen next time. There's a capricious element, a lot of luck involved. I feel 'This time I pulled it out of the hat. But next time, I may not.' "

One woman was at a loss to explain how she got her written reports done. She felt her analysis of the information came to her in some form of creative inspiration. Yet she didn't know how she was making this happen and felt that the process wasn't under her control.

The person who feels like an impostor has these doubts about his future success because he attributes his success to such things as timing, luck, or hard work. These are actually temporary, external, or irrelevant causes—they clearly can't be counted on in future efforts. How long can he get by, he wonders, on "easy" assignments, his glibness, flair, sense of humor, and so on? He imagines that each new project is finally going to be the one that leads to his exposure.

This can be an especially troubling thought for the person who works on his own, or in a business where he must continually pursue new assignments from different clients. He might be an independent corporate consultant, actor, writer, illustrator, or caterer. If he doesn't see himself as building on a solid foundation, then when he is done with one assignment, he will wonder if he'll ever work again.

If we are to have continued confidence in our future success, we must relate our success to internal, lasting causes. And that means intelligence, ability, and natural talents.

Statement #8. "I tend to feel like a phony."

A feeling of phoniness is the basic symptom of the Impostor Phenomenon. If you had a high score on this question, the feeling of phoniness is likely to be creating anxiety for you in some significant area of your life. However, you may feel phony in some specific situations, but not in others. And, you may feel phony *most* or *some* of the time in a particular role, but not at other times. How pervasive this feeling is depends upon how strong your "impostor" feelings are.

Think about exactly what it is that makes you feel like a phony. Do you exaggerate to others about your qualifications? Do you lie about your background? Do you say or do things that are false or misleading? Do you produce less than what you promise? If not, why do you feel you qualify as a phony? Have others usually been satisfied with your work or performance? In that case, do you think there's something wrong with *them?*

Do you believe it means you are a phony if you act one way, but feel another way inside? This is probably not phoniness, but a sense of your complexity and the unresolved contradictions we all feel.

Statement #9. "My personality or charm often makes a strong impression on people in authority."

If you scored 3 or above (in the direction of "Very true") on this statement, you may fall into the IP pattern of the Charmer. How much importance do you attach to your ability to win people over through the force of your personality? Do you believe your charm is the primary reason for your success? Have you ever tried to master a situation without using your asset of charm? (In other words, have you applied the theory of covariation I mentioned in Chapter 2? Do you experiment with cause-and-effect relationships like a scientist to see for certain if your charm is a necessary ingredient in your successes?)

One young woman who fits into this pattern works as an executive assistant. She told me that she felt the only thing she was good at was getting along with people socially. She had grown up feeling she couldn't possibly be very bright or qualified because she had little natural aptitude for math. This was an area her father excelled in, and he was always considered "the smart one" in the family. The fact that she was a good writer with an aptitude for languages meant little to her as she was growing up. In her mind, "smart" equaled "ability in math." Despite clear evidence that she was capable of the same level of work as her peers, feelings of incompetence remained with her in her work. She felt that her social skill was the only reason she retained her job.

Statement #10. "I consider my accomplishments adequate for this stage in my life."

If you answered in the direction of "Not at all true," you scored high on this question. You probably feel that you should have done a lot more with your life by now—no matter what age you are.

This is another feeling commonly shared by victims of the Impostor Phenomenon. A doctor of thirty-nine felt he should have been the head of his department in a major hospital by that point in his life. Since he was not, he was a failure in his own eyes. A housewife who had started college in her thirties felt she ought to finish a four-year program in one year. She felt she was inadequate because she compared herself to others her own age who had started college at eighteen and now had flourishing careers. Over and over, I hear victims of the Impostor Phenomenon tell me they have failed because they haven't yet reached "the top."

It certainly can be very satisfying to reach our goals at a relatively young age. It's satisfying to reach a goal at *any* age. But think about whether your standards for accomplishment are realistic. Most IP victims feel that no matter how high they rise, they haven't done enough. Despite his more than adequate career, a scientist told me he felt inadequate because he hadn't won the Nobel Prize by age fifty.

A desire to live up to an impossible ego ideal is to blame here. The yardstick by which many IP victims measure themselves is perfection. It is only with that perfection, universal knowledge, or complete competence that IP victims feel they would really be safe from the threat of exposure as a fraud. Rather than realizing that the ego ideal is an unattainable goal we can only strive toward, they literally attempt to reach it. When they don't, they feel as if they have failed.

Statement #11. "In discussions, if I disagree with my boss, professor, or the person in charge, I speak out."

If you found this statement "Not at all true" of you, you received a high score for this question. Do you tend to go along with the opinions or views of others? You may fall into the Chameleon IP pattern. Do you recognize yourself in the Chameleon's tendency to change his true colors in certain situations? Do you believe this approach helps you to feel safe from exposure as unqualified or inadequate? Said one woman: "I've always felt I've been able to fool people with my ability to mimic, to say what they're saying, to give them back information they already know."

As we've seen, the Chameleon's pattern is particularly difficult to break, because it actually involves some inauthentic behavior—pretending to believe in ideas or attitudes that don't agree with your own. In this way, the impostor self-image becomes even stronger.

Statement #12. "I often achieve success on a project, report, or test when I have anticipated I would fail."

This statement is "Very true" for some IP victims. These individuals are the Magical Thinkers, who are usually pessimistic when preparing for a performance event. They never feel fully confident that things will go well for them. It doesn't matter how positive their previous history has been under similar circumstances. For such a person, there is no carryover of confidence from past to future successes. Each new performance event is "the big one"—the significant test that may expose him as a fraud.

If you answered this question in the high IP direction, you may fall into this category. Has the fear of failure become a ritual for you that precedes every new task or important event? If you *don't* worry, do you feel a necessary part of your work has been left undone?

In reality, excessive worry is not constructive and contributes little to success. In fact, if it becomes too severe, it may psychologically disable you, making it impossible for you to concentrate on what you are doing. You can become too paralyzed with worry to act. Some IP victims relentlessly put themselves through self-punishing mental scenarios whenever they are preparing for a major event. Their visions are very real to them and allow them no peace.

Statement #13. "I often feel I am concealing secrets about myself from others."

A "Very true" answer here suggests strong IP feelings. People who experience strong feelings of fraudulence are aware of their feelings, but have great difficulty revealing them to others. They dread the consequences of making such a revelation. Their ultimate fear is that once they have shared their "impostor" secret, the other person will reply: "Yes, come to think of it, you really are a fraud. You had me fooled for a long time, but I can see you're not what you appear to be." A comment like this would be totally devastating for a victim of the Impostor Phenomenon.

There can be several kinds of secrets that IP sufferers believe they are concealing. They might be secrets directly related to work, such as, "I'm not really qualified for this job, even though they think I am." Or, they could have something to do with general intelligence: "They think I'm very wise because I only talk about things I know a lot about. Otherwise I just listen and *look* wise." Then there's "They don't realize I'm very glib, but I have no depth."

The secret might be something as general as a wish to be taken care of, instead of having to be in charge all the time. In her book *The Cinderella Complex,* Colette Dowling wrote at length about women's secret longings to depend on someone else.

Perhaps the IP victim wants to hide feelings of being socially inadequate. A woman who moved from her small Midwestern hometown to a large city said, "I thought they would eat me alive. I didn't know how to use chopsticks or say French words. I really felt I didn't belong here."

These secrets may revolve around specific personal roles. The person who appears "nice" to everyone all the time may feel he is hiding a darker side of his personality. His secrets are his occasional feelings of anger, jealousy or resentment. The young mother may have a different secret: she sometimes grows impatient with her toddler's constant need for attention. But, she feels, she couldn't uphold her reputation as a good mother if this secret should ever get out.

In the mind of an IP victim, his secrets are shameful ones. They must be concealed if he is going to ward off exposure and subsequent disaster.

Statement #14. "My public and private self are the same person."

Individuals with strong feelings of fraudulence frequently find this to be "Not at all true" for them. This statement goes to the heart of the IP victim's private conflict between his public image and his private image. Write down a description of your public image. Then describe your private image. See how the two contrast.

As we've seen, the research tells us that IP victims seem to experience a greater discrepancy between their public and private selves than do other people. They see themselves as inconsistent or "false." People without "impostor" feelings see themselves as simply responding to the demands of some situation in an appropriate fashion.

In Part II below, you'll be able to examine more closely any IP feelings you have and think about how you might display signs of the IP in your behavior. This should help you understand more about how the Impostor Phenomenon could be influencing you.

PART II

On a separate sheet of paper, write down your answers to the questions below. Think about each one for a while before answering. You are trying to uncover feelings that may be difficult to face and the answers may not come easily. Be as honest about your feelings as you can.

1. In what situation(s) do you feel like an impostor, fraud, or fake? Is it in relation to:

   ☐ your work
   ☐ your relationships with family members
   ☐ your relationships with friends
   ☐ your relationship with a lover or spouse
   ☐ social situations, such as parties
   ☐ some other area of your life

2. Why do you feel you're an impostor, fraud, or fake? (For example, do you believe you are un-qualified for your work, less intelligent or compe-tent than your peers or colleagues?)
3. What does it feel like to you to be an impostor or fraud? Describe the feeling.
4. Do you feel any of the following played a major part in your achievements? (List the appropriate one[s].)

   ☐ Good luck
   ☐ Charm
   ☐ Social skills
   ☐ Sense of humor
   ☐ Good looks
   ☐ Sexuality
   ☐ Family or business connections
   ☐ Effort
   ☐ Determination
   ☐ Other(s)

Do you believe any of the above have misled other people into overestimating your qualifications? How?

5. Do you find that your thoughts and feelings seem to conflict with what you say and do? In what way?

6. When you perform the role in which you feel like an impostor or fraud, how often do you have these feelings? All the time? Only in certain situations (and, if so, when)?

7. Do you worry that you'll be found out and exposed as a fraud? How much and how often do you worry about this?

8. What do you fear would happen if people "found out"?

9. What is it, or what do you think you do, that keeps people from "finding out"; why hasn't anybody "caught on"?

10. What are the *specific* things you do or ways in which you deal with other people to disguise the fact that you feel like an impostor? For example, do you always act self-confident? Do you assure others you can handle a task despite your own secret doubts about it? Do you engage in any of the behaviors of the IP "types," such as the Magical Thinker or the Chameleon? Do you work harder than everybody else? Do you try to charm other people? Do you try to win other people's approval, and, if so, how? Do you try to anticipate other people's psychological needs and be the person you think they want you to be?

11. How do you handle compliments or praise? Do you find it easy or difficult to accept other people's respect or admiration for you? Do you have a difficult time believing their evaluations of you? What do you usually say when others praise your accomplishments? Do you feel that they are simply too dumb to figure out the truth, or that you have manipulated or seduced them in some way?

12. Have you had these feelings in the past in other situations or other areas of your life? What were these situations?

13. If there were situations in the past when you had the feeling of being an impostor or fraud but *got over it*, what do you think enabled you to do so?

14. Do you have any ideas about why you feel like an impostor, despite the fact that you may *intellectually* understand how well you've done?

How It Happens—
In the Family

FIVE

By now you know what the Impostor Phenomenon is all about. You've seen how the feeling of being a fake can influence the way someone thinks and acts. You've had a chance to examine the roles you play, and consider whether the Impostor Phenomenon is affecting your life in some way.

But where do these feelings of fraudulence come from? Why do some people become victims of the Impostor Phenomenon while others do not?

There are many different reasons why someone might believe he or she is a fake. One answer can be found by looking back through time to the early years of childhood and the family situation. The dynamics among family members often spawn the most severe and persistent cases of the Impostor Phenomenon.

When the IP gets its start in childhood, it can be particularly difficult to shake. If a child begins to feel fake or fraudulent in some way, he wants to keep his family from finding out he is a "phony." He can adopt the same behavior as any other IP victim. He works diligently—too diligently—in school, at Little League practice, at his piano lessons. Or he worries constantly about failing at whatever he is trying to accomplish. If he senses that grown-ups find him charming and precocious, he plays up that side of his personality to win their approval. Compliments don't mean anything to him, unless he should stop receiving them. He can take on the Chameleon's style of copying others, or always try to act as he thinks his parents want him to. He puts up what he considers is a false front.

These ways of behaving only reinforce his feeling of phoniness. The Impostor Phenomenon now has a solid grip on him, and, over the years, becomes even more firmly entrenched.

Hilary is now thirty-three, a corporate executive who has risen quickly in her career. She remembers feeling like a fake even when she was a child. In her eyes, she was presenting a false image of herself as someone very bright and special. Her feeling was, "If I acted normally, my parents and my teachers wouldn't notice me, the other little girls wouldn't want me as their friend. I wasn't qualified to be average like the others, though I wanted that more than anything. So I created this persona of someone *above* average."

"My mother worked, unlike many mothers then," Hilary said. "When she came home, it was *showtime!* I felt I had to be special to get my parents' attention. I didn't act like a kid. I talked about books, art. I tried to get them to see me as this glamorous person."

Hilary believed she was creating illusions about herself for others. The feeling persisted throughout her youth and into adulthood, despite a string of impressive accomplishments. In school, she said, "I never felt I was scholarly. I was always the best student in the class, but I felt it was because I mimicked the teacher or the literature well, rather than having a solid basis of scholarly detail behind what I did. I always blamed it on having a good mimic's ear."

Certain kinds of family situations promote "impostor" feelings. However, the situation alone won't cause a child to feel like a fraud. Every child has his own inherent character traits. These traits play a part

150

in how much he is influenced by what goes on in the family. He may be walking through psychological land mines, but manage to emerge unharmed at the other end. Some children have resources outside their immediate families, which help them counteract "impostor" feelings. Teachers, friends, or a close aunt, uncle, or grandparent might make all the difference.

A child's family situation doesn't make it inevitable that he will become a victim of the Impostor Phenomenon. Still, it can set the stage with all the right props.

Where does it all get started?

FAMILY MYTHS AND LABELS

Early in life, a child is often assigned a particular role to play within his family. Based on something about his personality or abilities, he is given a label. He's known as "the smart one" or "the sensitive one." Maybe he's "the reliable one" or "the one with the personality." A child's label distinguishes him from the other members of his family and it can become an important part of his identity.[1]

If you ever read Louisa May Alcott's *Little Women*, you might remember that all four sisters in the book had very specific roles in the family. The oldest, Meg, was "the pretty one." Jo was the "tomboy" and "bookworm." Beth was known as the "peacemaker," and her father nicknamed her "Little Tranquility." The youngest, Amy, was "artistic," "selfish," and "vain."

One woman described to me how, as children, she and her sisters had assigned roles to themselves, just like the sisters in *Little Women*. So even if parents don't give out the labels, children sometimes do it on their own in order to establish their uniqueness.

Below are some of the labels—both positive and negative—commonly given to the different members

151

of a family. Do you recognize your own childhood role in any of them? Do they fit any of your brothers or sisters? Sometimes it's a parent or another close relative (aunt, uncle, cousin, grandparent) who is known as "the one with the sense of humor," "the creative one," and so on. Which one were you?

the smart one
the genius
the reliable or
   responsible one
the one with the
   sense of humor
the good one
the athletic one
the talented one
the spoiled one
the brat
the nice one
the understanding
   one
Daddy's girl
the "high-strung"
   one

the personality kid
the sensitive one
the good-looking one
the cute one
the clown
the caretaker or
   "little mother"
the creative or
   artistic one
the vain one
the slow one
the sweet one
the serious one
the tomboy
the dreamer

Whether a label is positive or negative, it may imply a whole world of meaning about what a child can—and can't—accomplish, and what role he is expected to play throughout life. The little girl who is always referred to as "poor Sally" may grow up pessimistically thinking of herself as deprived of something essential, not expected to accomplish very much. Whereas, Bobby, who was "born under a lucky star," will grow up expecting only good things to happen to him.

A child can run into trouble if his family focuses on his label and overlooks the other aspects of his personality. When he realizes he is always thought of as being one particular way, his label may become the most important part of his identity, and his role in the family becomes one-dimensional.

If his label is a positive one, the child may begin to rely heavily on playing that role as the way to win love and approval. His parents and siblings have come to expect him to act in a certain fashion, so he imagines that he had better not disappoint them.

When he doesn't want to, or can't, live up to his label, the child starts to doubt himself. "The one with personality" feels down one day, but knows he is supposed to show up at dinner with his usual smile. "The reliable one" is late getting home from school and panics because she promised to clean her room before Mom got home from work.

With so much of his identity invested in his role, the child is afraid to perform it in any way that is less than perfect. If something he does or feels conflicts with the role, he may feel that he really isn't what he seems. He doesn't deserve his special label. But, he thinks, if he lets his family know about his "weaknesses" and conflicts, they'll find out he's not the person they thought he was. They might not love him anymore. So he makes sure to hide his awful secret—that he is only a "fake."

If too much attention is focused on them, any of these labels can send a child on his way to becoming an IP victim. But the particular label he is assigned will determine which route he takes to get there.

THE SMART ONE

As a child, Nelson was very gifted in math. He recalled being told by his family that he was smart because he got good grades without having to work hard for them. His sister, they noted, also got high marks, "but she has to study." The implication was that his sister couldn't possibly be as bright as he was because she had to put so much effort into it.

Later in life, Nelson encountered some areas of study that were difficult for him, and he had to struggle to do well. He began to doubt whether he was really the genius his parents had thought him to be. But he kept his difficulties a secret so that he could preserve his family's image of him, as well as the gratification he got from that image.

If you were "the smart one," "the genius," or "the gifted one" in your family, you were probably expected to achieve a great deal. It may have been assumed you were going to say something smart or clever every time you opened your mouth. Perhaps you were told: "With your brains, you can be whatever you want to be" (which, in some cases, might have translated into "whatever *we* want you to be").

Living up to the label of "the smart one" can be a tough job. IP victims who grew up with this label often feel tremendous pressure to fulfill and sustain their family's image of them. They may go to great lengths to avoid disappointing the family. The only news they bring home has to do with their successes. When they are having difficulties, they suffer in silence, without asking for any emotional support. If they enter some kind of competition, they may not even tell the family until it's all over and they've clinched that first prize.

This role is so common to IP victims, it was one of the earliest to turn up in the research. When Clance and Imes did their first study of the Impostor Phenomenon among women, they found that many of those who felt like impostors had grown up as "the smart one."[2] This type of woman always felt pressure to live up to her image. She started to doubt herself when she came across situations where she had to struggle or work hard, instead of achieving perfection with ease. Reality was giving her the message that she wasn't truly the "genius" her family believed her to be. So she felt like an impostor.

These psychologists tell the story of one woman who was "the smart one" in her family. As a girl, she felt so pressured to maintain her family's image of her that she would stay home from school pretending to be sick on the days when spelling bees were held. She was afraid she wouldn't win and that would mean letting her family down.

Another woman, they found, used to hide her studying in childhood. When her mother came to her bedroom door, she pretended to be playing. She wanted to comply with the notion that she was a genius, and "geniuses don't have to study."

Sometimes, there is one particular area of study a "smart one" has trouble with and this becomes the true measure of success in his or her eyes. This is especially likely if an idealized or envied person in the family excels in that area. "The smart one" may be a whiz at history or music theory, but if his parent or sibling is good in science, then talent in science becomes the only mark of true ability to him.

When "the smart one" runs up against an area in which he doesn't meet with success easily, he sees it as evidence of his hidden incompetence. Like other people who believe they are impostors, he often sees his natural talents, aptitudes, or gifts—the things that come easily to him—as not counting *at all*.

THE SENSITIVE ONE

Perhaps you were known as the "sensitive" or "understanding" one. Maybe you were gifted with intuition, listening to everyone's problem and helping them to find solutions. This is also a very common childhood role among IP victims.[3]

Such children bring these qualities with them into adolescence and adulthood. They are the ones to whom friends come with problems. They can sympathize with the personal problems of their teachers, bosses, and mentors. People like them and think very highly of them.

Aside from being sensitive and understanding, these children may also be bright, talented, and creative. They would like to find some external recognition for those other qualities in themselves. Yet, when they receive that recognition, they begin to doubt its validity, and wonder if it's real. Because they've always been so adept at meeting other people's needs, they feel that what people are responding to is actually their understanding nature—not any real brilliance or competence on their part. Often, these IP victims had a brother or sister who was "the smart one," or the one groomed for higher education and a profession.

Because the sensitive or understanding one feels valued for that role, there is another way in which he or she can feel like a phony. Perhaps he isn't listening completely all the time to everyone's problems. As he gets older, he may find he's slightly resentful about being called by a depressed friend in the middle of the night or is secretly angry about having to sit through a litany of his boss's personal travails. Then he begins to wonder if even the image of him as being so sensitive isn't really a mistake.

THE CARETAKER

"The caretaker" is often an oldest sister or an only girl who puts the needs of others first. Even if she isn't assigned this role, she may create it for herself in order to feel needed, or to have a unique or special place in the family. Whether it is true or not, she feels that love and acceptance are based on her performing the caretaker's functions.

Becky, now twenty-seven, was a "caretaker" in her family. She is bright, articulate, and attractive, but these weren't the qualities she saw in herself as a child. Instead, she felt her value came from her nurturing of others. "I was a real good kid and I took care of everyone," she explained. "When I was a teenager, my mother had to work very long hours to support us, so I took care of my younger brothers and sister, and of her to a certain extent. I know now, and I knew then, without being able to articulate it, that that was the only role. If I didn't take care of everybody, they wouldn't love me."

THE CREATIVE, ARTISTIC, OR TALENTED ONE

The "creative" or "artistic" one may always be expected to be original or imaginative, to produce impressive work and come up with interesting ideas. With that kind of pressure, a child might very well start to worry that he can't sustain the role. Maybe next time, he thinks, the creative inspiration won't be there. The family and friends will be disappointed. Then where will his value lie?

If you were "the talented one" in your family, you were probably given dancing, acting, or music lessons. Did your parents used to call you out to the living room to sing or dance when they had company at the house? The talented child is often expected to perform well in public and make the family proud.

It can be rewarding and enjoyable to display one's talent, and the applause is something most talented children desire. However, if this dimension of a child is the only one that gets attention, too much of his identity comes to depend on performing perfectly and always hearing that applause.

The pressure grows. Now the child begins to wonder if he is talented enough to keep that applause coming. The idea of making an error, or giving a poor performance, fills him with dread.

Being on stage for one's family provides the opportunity for public admiration. But, in the case of a mistake or failure, it also entails the risk of a very public humiliation. The child who feels valued and loved for talent alone can magnify the consequences of one mistake into a disastrous failure.

This very situation takes place in a scene from the movie *Flashdance*. The family of a talented figure skater watches in pain and humiliation as she falls clumsily on the ice in front of a large crowd. The skater feels that she has let her family down. She decides that she isn't really talented after all and gives up her skating ambitions.

This role can cause other difficulties for a child. Some people draw a wide line between creativity or artistic talent, and intellectual ability. If a child sees himself only as an artist or performer, he might assume that he doesn't have "the brains" to hold his own in intellectual discussions.

As a young child, Dale was a star performer in her family and was known as "the spoiled one." "I was like a child prodigy because I used to sing and dance and all that stuff," she said. "I was precocious to some degree. But as I grew up and entered the world, I didn't think I was good enough. As a child in my own family, I was fine. But as soon as I got into the larger world, I became reserved to a large degree. I just didn't think I was smart enough."

THE PERSONALITY KID

Another role often found in families is that of "the one with the personality" or "the personality kid." This child is usually expected to be witty, warm, charming, extroverted, and fun—but often not especially intelligent, or headed for high achievement. When he gets good grades in school, they probably receive less attention, or are valued less, than those of the "smart" brother or sister.

It's as if only one child can be "the smart one" and one "the personality kid." If "the smart one" is outstanding at math, then the family believes that math is the measure of true genius. "The personality kid" may excel in languages or writing, and not in math. But these areas are not valued as highly by the family. When teachers praise the work of this child, his self-doubts set in. He figures that the teachers must be mistaken; they must have been taken in by wit and charm, leading them to overestimate his ability.

A pattern is set in motion. The child starts to imagine that praise and admiration aren't the result of his ability or intellect, but come from his likability. Others are only being fooled into thinking he is bright. This child grows up to be an IP Charmer.

A winning personality is a very positive asset. It only causes IP feelings if the role becomes one-dimensional. When this is the case, the child assumes he will only be valued by the family if he is "on" all the time. His intelligence and other skills are ignored, and he decides that he probably isn't very smart.

Curtis had always been a "personality kid" and was very well-liked by other people. Even the teachers who constantly had to reprimand him for talking during class had a soft spot for him. Curtis's intelligence was never emphasized by the family simply because it was eclipsed by his personality. It was his younger sister who got the label of "the smart one."

It came as a great surprise to Curtis when his sister barely passed her courses as a freshman in college. He not only graduated from college with honors, but was accepted to a prestigious graduate school in his field. According to his family's labels, this wasn't the way it was supposed to be.

Curtis also had another problem quite common for someone who has the role of "the personality kid." He became very depressed after breaking up with his girlfriend, but felt he couldn't share his sadness with anyone. If he did, he wouldn't be living up to the expectations of him as outgoing and full of fun. He felt compelled to stay alone in his room for hours, hiding from the world because he couldn't be his "usual self."

No one in Rachel's family denied that she was bright, but it was her younger brother who was "the genius." She had the warmth, charm, and sense of humor—a true "personality kid." Said Rachel: "There was a stated assumption that we were both bright. But my *brother!* He was a genius! I was told that about fifteen hundred times while I was growing up. Last year, my brother and I went to see a great-aunt we had never met before. We walked into the room and she immediately pointed at him. 'You're the smart one,' she said. 'Say something smart.' I wanted to murder her, but I still felt she was right."

THE GOOD-LOOKING ONE

Were you known as the "good-looking," "attractive," or "cute" one in your family? Physically attractive children are often admired and enthused over. "Isn't she adorable?" "He's going to break a lot of hearts when he grows up." "She'll never have trouble getting a date." Parents can place great emphasis on this child's appearance, fussing with his clothes and hair to show off the child's looks to even better advantage. They may constantly take pictures of their beautiful offspring, enter them in children's beauty contests, or take them on auditions for commercials. Little girls are told they will be prom queens and will grow up to be movie stars.

Sometimes this child picks up the message that he or she got the looks, and a brother or sister got the brains. Even though he may well be bright and competent, it isn't expected of him. He's so adorable—how could he be smart as well?

In adulthood, he may feel that his looks have opened doors for him; that he's had an unfair advantage over more qualified people. He knows he possesses the undisguisable advantage of physical attractiveness and wonders if he's ever really been tested on his ability alone. In personal relationships, he can feel he is loved only because he's so good-looking. He wonders if his looks have blinded his lover or spouse to those things about him that he sees as mediocre.

Earlier, I described how adults can feel like impostors about their appearance. One aspect of that was the feeling of having to hide behind a "mask" of cosmetics and clothes to appear more attractive. This problem can begin early in life if a child is naturally attractive. He can feel a powerful need to maintain a certain standard of beauty, because that always seemed to be the source of praise and love.

When an attractive person believes he depends on beauty to get by, it can be devastating to lose those good looks. Aging, or a disfiguring injury, may destroy his self-image and the self-confidence he has built up over the years. In his mind, his looks have become associated with success and acceptance.

THE GOOD ONE

Many people who feel like impostors as "nice people" have played the role of "the good one" or "the nice one" since they were children. Little girls might get the label of "Daddy's perfect girl" or "the sweet one."

Living up to any of these labels means never getting angry, always being a good listener, complying with your parents' every wish, and putting the needs of others ahead of your own. Sometimes the child takes on this role himself. He may believe he is compensating for a brother's or sister's deficiencies. By being good and nice all the time, he will make up to the parents for the one who has disappointed them.

Robin had the role of "the good girl." She did what her parents expected of her, including getting good grades. As she said: "I was a very good girl. I was expected to be—I had to be. And part of being a good girl was doing well in school." Yet, as a high school student, she had already begun thinking she might be fooling other people about her abilities.

"I had a teacher in high school who really liked me, and gave me all kinds of special assignments and different things to do," she recalled. "I couldn't quite figure out why. He thought I was really smart and it always scared me. I could never believe it. There weren't many teachers like that. He was an oddball in that school. He would call me at home and listen to the things I said.

"I had a friend with whom he had a similar relationship, who could get close to him, and who really got a lot out of the relationship. But I was never comfortable enough to get close to him. It always seemed like, why did he pick me? And I felt that if I really let him get close, then he would know he had made a terrible mistake."

Robin saw her good grades simply as another aspect of her "good girl" role, instead of a sign of unusual ability and intelligence. She described the teacher who found her bright enough to take a special interest in her as "an oddball." She was perplexed by his interest, feeling he had overestimated her brightness. She wasn't able to see herself as intellectually special and to confidently play protégée with her teacher. That kind of role involves receiving something for yourself. The role of "the good one" involves giving and complying.

162

If you're going to be the perfect "good one," you have to suppress your own anger, jealousy, selfishness, aggression, and rebelliousness. What an impossible job for a child! All of these emotions exist in any nice person. When they threaten to erupt, the result is great anxiety.

If "the good one" becomes conscious of having these negative emotions, she decides she hasn't lived up to the demands of her role. So she thinks other people have a high opinion of her simply because she is doing a good job of hiding her "ugly and bad" feelings.

Here is how Fern reflects on her years as the perfect "nice one." "It's not possible for anybody to be as nice as I was," she said. "During my childhood and teenage years I was really consciously 'nice.' I never got angry. I was always defending people whom other people attacked. Then, at one point I felt, 'I just can't do this anymore.' For the first time, I felt what it was like to get angry. And it terrified me out of my mind. I didn't even know what you *do* when you get angry.

"My suppression of things had to do with my role in my family. I was a *nice kid*. I was 'the nice one.' I was the one who always understood, who always was caring. This was part of my value. It was what made me different from my sister and brother. I was 'the one Mommy can always count on to be normal and calm,' 'the sweet one.' I eventually got defined that way."

Fern felt that discrepancy that goes along with seeing yourself as an impostor: her public reputation—being sweet, good, and calm—conflicted with her internal feelings. At one point, she developed a habit of coughing and clearing her throat repeatedly. This habit made her feel self-conscious and embarrassed. Finally it brought her to therapy. Her throat-clearing was a symptom of the underlying pressures of suppressing her anger. It was a signal to her. In time, she was able to get in touch with her feelings of anger. And she found the one solution to resolving that discrepancy: learning that basically good people can and do get angry, and that this doesn't mean they are terrible or evil, or will lose their identities.

WHAT THE CHILD DECIDES

When a child feels he is allowed to play only one role for the family, he has a hard time accepting the evidence that he has succeeded in other roles. It is difficult for him to see himself as flexible and multidimensional, capable of functioning well in more than one role. It feels wrong to him, and causes conflict and doubt.

As I've mentioned, a child doesn't always react to family role pressures by going along and then feeling fraudulent. Some children set out to prove their parents wrong.

A CEO who does *not* suffer from the Impostor Phenomenon told me how he views the family situation:

"I think parents recognize differences in their kids, but they don't realize how much they can increase, and even create, those differences. I was a second-born child. My older brother was always encouraged and rewarded, but I was not. Everything that a first-born does is noticed and rewarded by the parents— eating, smiling, walking, talking. When the first child throws up, the parents think it's just fantastic! With the second-born, it's all just a repeat performance.

"In school, I had difficulty fitting in. I had behavioral problems, I was punished for talking in class. But I think that a certain amount of insecurity can push people like me to be successful—to do what the world thought they couldn't do. For example, someone who gets scolded by the teacher can go out and prove that he is smarter than she is."

This man had become highly successful, much more so than his older brother. Despite his family history, there was something in his personality that made him certain he was qualified to succeed, and didn't lead to IP feelings about his sense of competence and ability to achieve.

On the other hand, some people force themselves into roles even when there's no family pressure to do so. And they torment themselves trying to live up to their self-imposed ideals.

Kim, in sales at a large manufacturing company in Ohio, had been under tremendous pressure preparing a major presentation for a client. She felt that her future within the company depended on how well the presentation went and that the result would be the true measure of her competence. She was overpreparing (part of the IP Workaholic's behavior), and complained of not knowing how well she was doing because there had been no feedback from her boss so far.

While all this was going on, she had been having attacks of panic: pounding of the heart, shortness of breath, feelings of heaviness in her arms and legs, and the fear that she would collapse. These episodes were so frightening that she visited a hospital emergency room twice, only to be told that nothing was physically wrong with her.

Kim had taken this job in a company far from home. She had worked in a gift shop for several years yet she wanted to achieve something more in life. Actually, her real interest was in writing, but she believed she *should* pursue a career in business.

It turned out that Kim had pushed herself in many ways throughout the years. She was known as "the adventuresome one" in her family. She was the only one to go away to college, instead of living at home and attending a local college as did her brother and sister. She had always thought of herself as an over-achiever, trying to do more than she was capable of and measuring herself against friends. When away at school, she had actually been very homesick. Now she was seeking a career in business because she felt this was what her father would have wanted.

As we traced her history, we realized that being only fourteen months younger than her sister had motivated Kim to establish herself as unique in some way within the family. She and her sister had always been close, played together, and been treated almost as twins. In her desire to differentiate herself, she had deliberately done things that were different from what her sister did, despite the fact that they weren't always comfortable or entirely natural for her. Because her sister went to college near home, she felt compelled to go away to school, simply to show she was different and to maintain her reputation as adventuresome.

When Kim actually made her presentation, she did an excellent job. Yet she found the experience anticlimactic; her overpreparation and anxiety had totally exhausted her. In Kim's case, the panic attacks were anxiety symptoms, signals that she was leading her life to accommodate the requirements of a certain role, rather than in the way she really wanted. Her symptoms cleared up when she moved back to her hometown and pursued the career she really wanted.

ROLES AND REALITIES

It can be very revealing to compare family labels to what everyone in the family is doing today.

Did all your other family members live up to their labels? Did "the smart one" in your family actually get the best grades? Who has gone the furthest in his education? Who has the highest-paying job? The most glamorous or interesting job? Who do you think has become the most successful?

Have you continued to play the role you were assigned in your family? Or have you dared to venture outside of it and allowed yourself to expand beyond that role? Have you shown your family and friends that there is more than one important dimension to your character? Are you able to see yourself as a multidimensional person whose value doesn't depend upon being successful at a single role? Can you allow for a less-than-perfect performance from yourself in a role?

Do the realities fit the roles, or are the roles an illusion that the family needs to preserve? It is interesting to see who you are today in relation to who you were as a child in your family.

CRITICISM AND APPROVAL

For some IP victims, the big childhood issue was not about playing one or another specific role. It was all about criticism. Nothing they did was ever good enough for their parents. And because they accepted their parents' impossible standards, as adults, they can never do well enough to suit themselves.

Very early in childhood, we develop either a sense of certainty or a sense of doubt about whether we are competent, so it's important that parents encourage and praise a child's attempt to master new situations. Maneuvering up and down steps, feeding himself, putting on his own clothes—no matter how well or poorly he first does it, any efforts a child makes at such things should be praised by his parents.

Unfortunately, this doesn't always happen. Sometimes, a parent projects his or her own feelings of inadequacy onto the child. In some cases, the parent may also feel ambivalent about any move toward independence by the child and may act to discourage this. The parent focuses only on the flaws in the child's performance; anything short of perfection is unacceptable.

There is one story that a number of IP victims have told me about themselves. As children, they brought home a report card with four A's and a B. The only response they got from a parent was: "What's that B doing there?" It didn't matter if the B was in science or gym. In the parent's eyes, it made the child less acceptable.

In some families, it isn't the parents who are critical of the child. Instead, a brother or sister (usually older) is the one who belittles everything the child tries to do. The older sibling may or may not realize what he is doing. In some cases, he is only being blunt in the way that children often are. But if the younger child looks up to that sibling, the criticism can be just as piercing as if it had come from a mother or father.

As adults, IP victims often carry this critical voice within themselves. They have internalized it in the form of self-criticism. When they observe themselves being successful, that voice begins to raise doubts, questioning whether the success is real or merely an illusion.

When Valerie was growing up, she wanted to be an actress or a model. But her mother continually implied that she was "vain" and "an exhibitionist." She internalized her mother's critical voice, so, as an adult, felt very uncomfortable about expressing herself or trying to make herself look attractive. The mother's voice inside her made Valerie believe that such efforts meant she was arrogant and would be ostracized by others. Although Valerie is now a successful political lobbyist she still devalues her own achievements.

Rosemary is a bright and attractive young lawyer in Phoenix, doing well in her job. Yet she never felt that she was smart or competent. As she was growing up, her parents had continually told her she wasn't very smart and probably couldn't handle the pressures of an academic education.

Her parents' criticisms were compounded by an experience Rosemary had in school when she was quite young. Her second-grade teacher decided that Rosemary should skip the third grade and go straight from second grade to fourth. The pressures of suddenly being in with more advanced children caused Rosemary so much anxiety that she couldn't concentrate on her schoolwork. And she was aware that her father—who was thought of in the family as a "genius"—felt that Rosemary wasn't good enough to skip ahead in school. She also felt tremendous pressure to meet the expectations of the teacher who had shown such faith in her by suggesting the move.

Rosemary was so ridden with conflict and anxiety that her performance in school suffered, and she lost all confidence in herself. To make matters worse, the teacher took her aside one day and said, "I'm very disappointed in you. I'm putting you back in the third grade." She was terribly humiliated. Yet, once back with the children in her old group, she was no longer anxious, and felt safe enough to perform well once again.

Many years later, Rosemary was able to realize that her father was a very immature and competitive man. Even though she was just a small child, he was penalizing his daughter for succeeding in intellectual pursuits—"his" area of expertise. Rosemary had to avoid being too successful in school if she was to escape being punished by his scathing, sadistic brand of criticism.

When it came time for college, Rosemary's teachers

advised that she apply to one particular top school. They were certain that she would be accepted and could win a scholarship to cover the costs. Her best friend was applying there and she became very excited over the prospect of the two of them going to school together. But her parents refused to give their permission, saying that "she wouldn't be able to handle the pressure." Her friend was accepted and went off to school without her. Rosemary went to a small local college, where she became quite depressed. She began to believe that her teachers were wrong and her parents were right—she probably wasn't very smart after all.

Surprisingly enough, Rosemary continued to do well in school, even though her father had done his best to make her doubt her intellectual abilities. She even went on to law school. However, when she did excel in her courses, she always felt anxious because of her old fears that her father would retaliate against the competition. And she tended to devalue whatever she accomplished.

A parent doesn't have to *speak* his words of criticism; through his actions or attitudes, he can impart the message of disapproval just as effectively. As a twenty-six-year-old journalist recalled: "My parents' encouragement wasn't honest to me. They never put me down—it was their lack of trust in me. When I was a teenager, they were very strict; they treated me like a child. That influenced me. If people don't trust you, you feel like you're going to do something wrong."

The child who grows up with constant criticism may become very anxious as an adult about any outward sign of success—be it a promotion, money, or some other public form of recognition. He fears that any successful performance will be carefully scrutinized because it "stands out." He also fears that if he is openly proud of his successes, his humiliation will be even worse when some flaw is discovered. His worry is that "pride goeth before a fall."

And he always feels certain that a flaw will indeed be found. He has adopted his parents' critical voices as his own, so he doesn't believe he can possibly have done a good job. He becomes his own worst critic. After any success, he immediately focuses on the weaknesses in his performance. Others may never notice these things, but he remains afraid they will discover that he has only fooled them into believing he is perfect.

WHOSE APPROVAL COUNTS?

Some IP victims have a history of receiving approval from one parent, and criticism from the other. The one parent always gives them praise for their accomplishment, talents, and gifts; the other has nothing but harsh words about anything they are trying to do.

When a child hears two strong parental voices—one approving, one disapproving—who is he to believe? IP victims usually doubt the judgment of the approving parent and feel that the critical parent is the one whose approval they *must* have. He or she is the one "who counts." In some cases, the child wavers back and forth, torn over whose opinion of him he should believe.

Denise was the child of an approving, accepting father and a mother who always criticized her. Although she was very pretty and bright, Denise couldn't do anything right in her mother's eyes. If she did well in school, her mother said nothing. She never even encouraged her to think about going to college.

When Denise became popular with the "in" group at school, she was informed by her mother that if she were really a nice person, she would be spending more time with the "outsiders."

Denise's mother had a long list of the things that she felt were wrong with her daughter. Denise was lazy, arrogant, and demanding. And if she didn't go along with her mother's demands, she was "not a good daughter."

On the other hand, Denise's father was always pleased with his child and very accepting of her. But that approval didn't count for much in her eyes. As a grown woman, when she received approval from men, she judged them to be "fools."

When IP victims grow up seeking the approval of a parent, they tend to displace this need for approval onto the people who judge them in adulthood. As adults, they are forever searching for their mother's or father's acceptance in the words of others. But even when they find acceptance from others, it's not enough. A substitute is just that. No one else can be "the real thing"—a disapproving parent suddenly turned accepting. They imagine that those experts who give them praise, recognition, or awards must be undiscriminating and easily fooled. Those who withhold the reward must be the ones "who count." Over and over again, they experience feeling deprived of approval.

Intellectually, IP victims know that qualified experts aren't so easily fooled. But, emotionally, they can't fully believe in the approval they get. The influence of the disapproving parent leaves its mark during that critical period when the child's sense of mastery first develops.

OVERPRAISING

Some IP victims say that they were never criticized by their parents. Instead, they were constantly praised. Sometimes—but not always—they grew up as only children. Anything they were or did was always "the best, A-number-one, wonderful."

As children, these people heard some grandiose assessments of their gifts or abilities. According to their parents, they weren't just bright, they were "brilliant." Not just attractive, but "a raving beauty." A talented child became "a child prodigy." A good athlete turned into "a natural champion." The parents went way beyond focusing on some label they had given their child. They idealized some aspect of the child so they could all share in something extraordinary.

In some cases, parents do this because they themselves were criticized as children, so they try too hard to act differently with their own children. More often, though, the whole family is searching for a way to feel special.

A family's expectations for such a child are extreme. They tell him, "You'll win the Nobel Prize someday"; "You'll become Miss America"; "You'll be a famous movie star . . . a major-league player . . . an Olympic winner . . . a millionaire." The child believes this for a time. But when he goes out into the world, he gets a rude shock. Suddenly he sees how difficult it is to achieve such an unrealistic ideal and how much work it takes.

This child also has to face two painful realities about himself. First, he discovers that he was simply a big fish in a small pond—there are plenty of other equally qualified people in the world going after the same thing he is. Second, he realizes that many of the steps on the road to success must be taken alone. His efforts won't always be rewarded with praise and admiration. He may not get any feedback at all, or worse, other people might actually criticize him when he doesn't do well. He's not used to this. It's a new and miserable experience for him.

Sometimes this person is in the kind of job where there is no one else to tell him how he's doing. The only validation he is going to get must come from himself. But he hasn't been raised to listen to his own opinions or to base his self-concept on his own judgments and feelings. The source of his positive feelings about himself have always come from the opinions of others. He may go out of his way to find a mentor who will give him the validation his family always provided. He needs the praise and admiration of an "expert."

This individual is a perfect candidate for the Impostor Phenomenon. When the praise and admiration he is accustomed to aren't forthcoming, he can begin to feel like a fraud. He feels successful *only* when he is being praised. When he is criticized, or doesn't get any feedback at all (which is probably a good deal of the time), he thinks he is a complete failure.

The idea of failing—which in his mind means being anything less than the best—is terrifying to him. If he doesn't fulfill his "destiny," he is afraid he will lose his family's love. But he now knows that he is merely *one* of the best, not *the* best. He feels he must "pretend" in public that he still deserves his old image as the best, thus making himself feel fraudulent. Any kind of mistake may reveal him as a fake, causing not only his own failure, but also the humiliation of the entire family.

THE NARCISSISTIC PARENT

Another pattern in the family history of IP victims is one in which the parents were overly helpful and overprotective. The parents intruded on the child's life so much that he began to doubt he could manage on his own.

As adults, these IP victims are afraid they can't perform their roles without the help of a mentor or supervisor. They crave feedback and have little feeling for how to judge themselves realistically.

What has usually happened in this case is that one or both parents have been too involved in the child's achievements. This involvement is a narcissistic one; that is, it had to do with the parent's concern for himself. The parent was a perfectionist who saw the child's performance as a reflection of himself. So he could never allow the child to tackle a project alone, in case the child should make a mistake.

This sort of parent may reveal his self-concern by the way he gets involved in his child's homework. He scrutinizes it to make certain it is absolutely correct. When there are math problems to be done, he "helps," saying, "Do it this way," instead of letting the child figure it out for himself. If an essay has to be written, the parent corrects the most minute spelling and punctuation errors; he may go so far as to rewrite sections, or even write it all in the first place.

All this is done in a seemingly helpful way. But, in truth, the parent is personally anxious about the child's image. He treats the child as an extension of himself, as a reflection of his own image. The parent doesn't want the teacher to see any flaws in the child's work, because somehow this will reveal a flaw in *him*—he has produced a child who is less than perfect.

Keith was an excellent writer, but developed a great

anxiety about his skills in this area. He recalled that his father had always written his school papers with him. In college, his father had practically written his senior thesis for him, focusing obsessively on every detail.

When Keith was on his own as an adult, he felt that he wasn't capable of good writing. He became acutely anxious whenever he had to write a report for his job, or even prepare a memo. He was afraid he wasn't qualified to do these things and had simply misled the people who hired him. He would feel anxious in his job unless someone was available as a supervisor or mentor to approve of his work and validate his performance. Keith had been raised with the message "You can't do it alone."

Sometimes a parent will focus his or her concern on the child's appearance. Often, this is a mother who views her daughter's appearance as an extension of her own. So the little girl's attractiveness becomes an issue of great importance to the mother. She may carefully dress her daughter (sometimes throughout the girl's adolescence), picking out her clothing, fixing her hair, and applying her makeup for her.

When this daughter grows to be an adult, she may feel she can't make herself attractive on her own. She lacks the confidence to buy her own clothes without the approval of a friend. Before she goes anywhere, she must have someone reassure her that her hair and makeup are satisfactory. If she doesn't get this validation, she feels anxious and self-conscious. She imagines that she isn't qualified to be an adequate judge of her own appearance.

Liza, a graduate student in biology, had grown up with a mother who had denied herself the status career she really wanted. Instead, her mother lived vicariously through Liza's achievements. In college, Liza was able to do brilliant work as long as her advisor was available. Despite her excellent qualifications, when it came time to go off on her own, she felt incapable of functioning by herself.

THE FEAR OF SUCCESS

I know I've talked a great deal about the fact that people who feel like impostors are afraid of failure. Just the thought of it makes their blood run cold. But, paradoxically, many of them can also unconsciously be afraid of success. Often, they are aware only of feeling anxious, but don't know why—everything is going so well. They don't connect that feeling with the idea that they are afraid to succeed. Nor do they realize that these periods of anxiety are related to situations associated with the possibility of success.

This is another aspect of the Impostor Phenomenon that can get its start in childhood.

Why would anyone be afraid of success? Isn't success what all the struggling is for? In our jobs, our love affairs, our friendships—success is what we're always after. Or so we would think.

Success may be desirable, but it can hold great terrors for us as well. Think about what it means to pursue success. Every situation that holds the potential for success also holds the potential for failure. When we decide to take on a task, we know that it can result in either one of these two outcomes. So if we dare attempt to succeed, we put ourselves in a position that may also lead to failure. The person who feels like a fake is well aware of the gamble he takes when he sets out to achieve.

What happens if we actually should succeed? An IP victim fears that the higher he goes, the harder he will fall. Each time he climbs another rung on the ladder of success, he sees the stakes getting bigger. He now fears a failure of an even larger magnitude and a more widespread public humiliation. He is afraid he will suffer the same fate as a classic tragic hero, plunging from great heights of glory to the depths of despair.

There are many reasons why IP victims—and others—are afraid of success. Some fear the pressures of success, worrying that other people will expect them to take on even more responsibilities. Or they may be afraid that they will become the object of resentment and envy; others might jealously compete with them or sabotage them in some way.

Then there is the visibility that can come with success. People who feel they are impostors may fantasize about fame, but they become highly uncomfortable when actually in the limelight. In the center stage of success there are many pairs of eyes to focus on every imperfection. There is safety in remaining obscure, back in the shadows where imagined flaws can more easily be hidden.

Those who surpass the achievements of their family members may be afraid that "it's lonely at the top." They fear a psychological separation from their families, worrying that they will become outsiders to their relatives and old friends. They can feel guilty about their success as well, thinking that it's somehow wrong for them to be doing better than a parent or sibling. A woman may feel guilty about having a college education or professional career because her mother never had the opportunities for these things. Or a man may feel guilty about making more money than his father because this implies he has somehow eclipsed his father's position in the family.

The fear of success can penetrate our personal lives as well. A woman may feel guilty about having a happy love relationship if her own mother was unhappy in marriage. The man whose brother is shy and withdrawn might restrain himself from becoming too popular. In friendships or romantic relationships, some people may fear that others will place too many pressures or responsibilities upon them. They may also shy away from "successful" intimacy because it would allow someone else to get too close on an emotional level.

The idea that some people fear success is not a new one. In 1926, Sigmund Freud wrote about the guilt and anxiety that may be associated with success.[4] In an earlier essay, "Those Wrecked by Success," Freud talked about the paradox of people falling ill just at the time a long-cherished wish was coming to fulfillment.[5] He proposed that some wishes or fantasies are fine as long as they *remain* wishes or fantasies. But once they threaten to become a reality, we may have to find a defense against them.

Freud's example of illness as a reaction to success is one example of a defense against the fear of success. Someone who fears success must find a way to protect himself against his fear. He needs a psychological defense for protection. He doesn't voluntarily or consciously set up this defense; his unconscious mind does it for him.

Psychological defenses aren't necessarily bad. They can be a helpful way of adapting to difficult or stressful situations and emotions. But they become a problem if they keep us from functioning and are hurtful to us in some way.

One defense against the fear of success is literally not to succeed. Some people stay away from any situation that could lead to success. Others make the effort to achieve, but somehow sabotage themselves. Without knowing why, they find themselves procrastinating until it's too late to do a good job on that report or presentation, or they miss the deadline altogether. They can unwittingly ruin their own opportunities, maybe by forgetting an important interview or appointment. Or they might inhibit their competitiveness enough to keep them from accomplishing as much as they are really capable of.

Another defense against the fear of success is to attain success in reality, but find some way to deny it in your own mind; one way people can deny their successes is by believing they are impostors.

Anyone can avoid his fear of success if he believes he is getting ahead through fraud, rather than through his own abilities. He's not aware of this mental process, but it's as if he's telling himself, "I'm not *really* a successful person. I'm just a phony who's been fooling other people. So it's okay for me to be doing so well at this."

In *Success and the Fear of Success in Women,* Dr. David Krueger, a professor of psychiatry at Baylor College of Medicine, wrote about how women can "erode" their accomplishments through the Impostor Phenomenon by undoing compliments and explaining their success as being due to luck, accident, or circumstances.[6]

For both men and women, the Impostor Phenomenon can be an unconscious defense against the fear of success. If we see our success as just a fluke, we know we're not a serious competitor or a threat to anyone. We can't be "blamed" for our success or held responsible for it. The fear of failure, which troubles so many IP victims, is actually masking a fear of success in some cases.

A common description of the fear of failure and the fear of success is as two sides of the same coin. Being afraid to fail is something we can understand and accept in ourselves. Who would want purposely to fail? But the idea that we might be afraid to succeed is harder for us to understand, and it is tied up with powerful and frightening emotions. So we disguise it as the fear of failure.

As Dr. Krueger put it, the fear of failure is "a rationalized fear of success, made consciously understandable." A fear of failing, then, may really be an unconscious *wish* to fail—or, at least, a wish *not to succeed*.

THE OEDIPAL CONFLICT

We've looked at many of the reasons people fear success. They can be afraid of the pressures and responsibilities. They don't want to be caught in the "spotlight" of success where all their flaws will be visible to the world. Maybe they feel they shouldn't be more successful than their parents, or a brother or sister; they fear a psychological separation from their families.

Another idea about why some people fear success is based on Freud's theory of the Oedipal phase of childhood. In Greek mythology, Oedipus, the son of a king and queen, was left to die in the mountains after a prophet predicted he would grow up to kill his father and marry his mother. Rescued by shepherds, he grew to adulthood and unknowingly fulfilled the prophecy. A stranger on the road whom he had quarrelled with and killed turned out to be his father; the widowed queen he then married was later revealed to be his own mother. When he discovered what he had done, the shame and horror were so great for him, he blinded himself.

Freud believed that Oedipus had acted out a wish or fantasy that everyone in every culture has in early childhood. He called this phase of development—normally between the ages of three and five—the Oedipal phase. At this time, a little boy wants to have his mother's care, love, and attention exclusively for himself. He may talk about wanting to "marry

Mommy," and wishes Daddy would go away or die so that he could replace him in his mother's affections. A little girl has the same feelings in reverse: she wants to have Daddy to herself and wishes that her rival, Mommy, would disappear.

Of course, at this age, children don't understand the notions of incest or death. However, they are frightened by these aggressive, competitive instincts in themselves. They are also in conflict because a part of them is afraid to win the victory that would make their wishes come true.

Even though the little boy wants to take his father's place with mother, he doesn't want to lose his father's love and protection. If he were to get his wish and win Mother all for himself, his father might abandon him or, even worse, retaliate. His father's revenge would be terrifying—perhaps he would even castrate the little boy. The little girl realizes that she needs her mother's protection and care. If she were to win Daddy away, Mother might abandon her or angrily strike back. Because winning would entail loss and punishment, victory is seen as being full of conflict, accompanied by powerful and overwhelming emotions.

Some children are aware of their wishes to have one parent all to themselves and vanquish the other parent, but they keep their wishes secret. Others express them out loud. "Daddy, why don't we go away together and leave Mommy here?" a little girl may ask. Parents often notice how their three-year-olds enjoy climbing into bed between them, separating them from one another.

This situation is resolved as the child begins to identify with the parent of the same sex. The little boy gives up his rivalry with his father, replacing it with a wish to be like him and to have a wife of his own in the future. He comes to understand that he can get for himself what his father has. The little girl realizes that she wants to be like her mother and that someday she can have her own husband. Children give up their Oedipal wishes and the memory of them becomes buried deep in the unconscious mind.

However, if something goes amiss in the child's psychological development, the child grows up without having resolved these wishes and fears. Then the idea of success—in school, at work, or in relationships—can become associated in the unconscious with the old Oedipal issues. "Winning" is still tied up with the idea of winning the competition with the same-sex parent for the love of the other parent. Another way of looking at it is that the person feels guilty about his or her incestuous feelings towards the opposite-sex parent. This brings on all the frightening emotions that went along with this conflict in childhood.

As an adult, this person is now afraid of the penalties of success. With every possibility for success, he is unconsciously reliving his guilt over wanting to have sexual relations with one parent and do away with the other—and the fear of punishment that may result if he achieves this goal.

It's my belief that the Impostor Phenomenon is also a defense against a fear of success associated with Oedipal conflicts. Again, one can deny his victories by believing he is only a fake who has fooled other people.

Such emotions are seldom in our awareness as adults. Most of the time they lie repressed deep in the unconscious. People who enter psychoanalysis, however, are often able to get in touch with these powerful emotions and memories.

Henry is a sixty-four-year-old attorney who had gone into psychoanalysis. On the analyst's couch one day, he began to remember the Oedipal stage of his

183

development. Henry was an only child, and his father's work had frequently taken him away from home. During his father's absences, Henry enjoyed being his mother's "helper" around the house. He recalled wanting to have her love, both physical and emotional, all to himself. When he was three, he attempted to poison his father by placing a few drops of rubbing alcohol in his father's food.

When these childhood memories came back to Henry, he felt like a fraud—a murderer and a rapist in the disguise of a respected, successful lawyer. Around the same time, he had also been having anxiety during the act of making love. He realized that he felt making "love" was fraudulent for him; that it was not love at all, but an act associated with murderous, aggressive wishes.

WHO MUST PAY FOR YOUR SUCCESS?

The fear of success can also be tied into the idea that our success means someone else's loss. Some people are unconsciously guilty because they believe their victories are coming at the expense of another.

Nicole, thirty, spoke of her extreme anxiety and guilt whenever she took a step toward success. She would have to "sneak up on herself" and accomplish things very quickly and quietly to prevent this feeling from completely paralyzing her progress. Throughout life, she tended to downplay her achievements in academics, athletics, and her work as a project manager in a government agency. Each of these areas caused her anxiety and guilt to surface. She believed she was a fraud who didn't deserve to enjoy any form of success. In denying her accomplishments, her "impostor" feelings only grew worse.

In therapy, Nicole was able to trace the development of her feelings of fraudulence. For one thing, she hadn't resolved her Oedipal feelings about surpassing her mother. But there was something else that was holding her back as well.

Nicole was able to recall a repressed memory of her female relatives talking about a miscarriage her mother had had before Nicole was born. She had always thought of herself as the oldest child in the family—the first-born. Now she saw that her mother had lost a child who "should" have been the first-born.

Nicole had grown up with the feeling that her position as the oldest child wasn't rightfully hers and had only been achieved at the expense of someone else's life. She sobbed bitterly when she recalled all this, saying, "Somebody else had to die in order for me to live." The family secret had been so painful that it was never openly discussed or explained. This left Nicole with a distorted picture of her own right to exist. Unconsciously, she felt everything she achieved was fraudulent, because her very life wasn't deserved. Nicole had associated any victory with the death of another.

Malcolm also saw his success as coming at the expense of someone else. He had been physically abused by his parents as a child, but was finally able to escape from home by going away to college on a scholarship. While at school, he became convinced he was a fraud, and suffered extreme anxiety because of it.

Malcolm's parents had always told him he could never accomplish anything worthwhile in life and this was certainly one reason he questioned his achievements. But Malcolm was also feeling guilty about having left his younger brother behind to suffer the parents' abuse. In the past, he had always functioned as his brother's protector, shielding him from their mother and father as much as he could. By going away to school, he felt he had saved himself and abandoned his brother.

In Malcolm's mind, he had used academic accomplishments to improve his own life at his brother's expense. His guilt-ridden desire to escape from a painful family life made him feel his achievements were fraudulent. His grades, awards, and scholarship became symbols of his terrible deed.

Casey had always been told by his parents to downplay his talents and intellect, because his younger brother wasn't very bright, and Casey's achievements would "hurt his feelings." This brother was the parents' favorite child, and they overprotected him at Casey's expense. Casey began to keep his interests to himself and became a loner with a secret fantasy life. He could allow himself to be successful or famous only in his fantasies.

Casey felt immense anger and jealousy toward his brother. But he hid his feelings, and even pretended to be inept when he was around his parents in the hope that he might someday win their love and acceptance. He secretly felt that he wasn't a loving person because he so deeply resented the role he was forced to play. Having to conceal his real desires, emotions, and abilities all contributed to his feelings of fraudulence.

Some children have handicapped brothers or sisters whom they feel must be protected from feeling inadequate. Even when parents try very hard to prevent it, these children may feel that their accomplishments are hurting the less fortunate sibling. Their guilt leads them to give up on achieving, or to try to deny their success in some way.

This feeling of having achieved at a price to someone else can have sources other than one's family. Sometimes people feel guilty because they attribute anything good that happens to them to their own good luck in the face of other people's misfortunes. I have noticed this among veterans of the Vietnam war who have managed to reestablish solid family lives and careers. Often, they feel that "the ones who really deserve it" died in Vietnam. Underlying every success is a feeling that it has been achieved at the expense of the dead or disabled.

Jared was a veteran of this war. After attending a support-group meeting for Vietnam veterans, he came away feeling even more guilty and more undeserving than before. Most of the men at the meeting were unemployed, trying to recover from failed marriages, addicted to drugs, or disabled by traumatic stress.

Jared saw his success as merely a matter of luck or fate; it was only accident that he too had not been struck down in some way. He felt like an impostor because he saw himself as undeserving of his own good fortune. He wondered why he should be entitled to more than others who had been killed or injured.

Whatever the reason someone fears success, he may begin regarding himself as an impostor as an unconscious form of psychological protection. It is a safe escape route whereby he can continue to achieve without having to "admit" to himself how much he's accomplished.

How It Happens—In the World Around You

SIX

I made good in spite of myself, and found to my dismay, that Business, instead of expelling me as the worthless impostor that I was, was fastening upon me with no intention of letting me go.

—*George Bernard Shaw*, Selected Prose

As we've seen, the feeling of being a fake often gets its start in the dynamics of a family situation. However, in the world outside the family, there are a number of other circumstances that can lead someone to feel he is an impostor. These other circumstances can be social, cultural, or simply tied in with the situation itself.

NEW ROLES

I've mentioned that "impostor" feelings can be brought on when we move into a new and unfamiliar role. For one person, that might mean going off to school; for another, getting that big promotion. It could mean having a child and becoming a first-time parent. Perhaps a woman is entering the work force for the first time after being a full-time homemaker for many years. We don't yet know how to handle the role and may then decide that we're not qualified to play it at all. In any of these cases, the Impostor Phenomenon can take hold and persist. Or it may pass with time as we become more comfortable with the situation.

In their research on the Impostor Phenomenon, several psychologists have looked at the connection between feelings of fraudulence and new roles. Earlier, I talked about a study I did to measure the IP in college juniors and seniors. Half of those students were in an honors program, and their average group score on the Harvey IP Scale was higher than that of the students who were not doing honors work.

In 1984, Michael Penland and Dr. Susan McCammon also did a study of college students, and compared their findings with mine.[1] In their study, 57 male and female freshmen and sophomores at a Southern university filled out the Harvey IP Scale. These students were all candidates for honors programs, with grade point averages of at least 3.5. They had yet to decide if they wanted to accept the invitation to do honors work at school.

The students in Penland's and McCammon's study scored even higher on the IP Scale than had my junior and senior honors students. This suggested they had not one, but two, factors that made them predisposed toward stronger feelings of fraudulence. First, even though the students in my study were dealing with the effect of being publicly recognized as successful, at least they had a couple of years of college already under their belts. The freshmen and sophomores in Penland and McCammon's study were newer to the basic college situation and the role of college student.

Secondly, as Penland and McCammon pointed out, the sample of students they surveyed hadn't yet accepted the honors program invitation; they may have felt even more uncertain than my sample about whether they were qualified or intelligent enough to handle the work. We can imagine the questions running through the minds of those students with "impostor" feelings: "Has the school made some mistake in asking me to do honors work?" "If I join the honors program, will I be revealed as a fraud in front of *really* bright students?" All around, this opportunity could be a frightening proposition for a bright student who has secret doubts about his abilities.

I had also taken my original study one step further to show how new situations can intensify feelings of fraudulence. I compared the IP scores of the 26 senior honors students with those of more advanced students—18 first-year students in graduate school.

The average IP score for the first-year graduate students shot up more than 8 points over that of the undergraduate honors students. In terms of statistics, this difference was significant; it was too big a jump to be random or coincidental.

A first-year graduate student is, of course, more educationally advanced than any undergraduate student, honors program or not. We might think that, having been accepted into graduate school, a student could relax and stop worrying about his qualifications. He has made it into the upper reaches of academic study. Yet, acceptance into graduate school—objective evidence of achievement—didn't help to ease IP feelings in this group. Just the opposite: It seemed to provoke a stronger IP experience.

These first-year graduate students were facing a new situation in which they felt they had to prove themselves all over again as qualified and capable. Even at this higher level of achievement, the sheer newness of being low man on the totem pole seemed to increase vulnerability to IP feelings.

At the same time, I also gave this test to graduate students in their second, third, and fourth years of school. The average score of second-year graduate students was 11 points *lower* than that of the students just starting the program. It appears that, in general, by the second year of graduate school, a student is more comfortable with his role and feels more like he belongs in the group. Here, the intensity of "impostor" feelings diminished. They were getting accustomed to performing their roles as graduate students.

There was more food for thought, however. The average scores began to rise for students in the last two years of graduate school. I believe these students were beginning to feel apprehensive about presenting their doctoral dissertations, finishing school, and receiving their academic degrees—critical performance events. This public acknowledgment of success might again provoke fears of exposure ("Will they give me my degree or will they discover I faked my way through the program?"). Also, these students may have been worrying about the next step in their careers—leaving the student role behind and placing themselves in another new situation they would soon have to master.

In 1983, Dr. Mary Topping had surveyed those 285 faculty members and found that lower-ranking professors had stronger IP feelings than the more established, higher-ranking ones. This suggested that the newer professors were struggling to learn their new roles and adopt them as part of their self-images.

All these studies are creating a kind of seesaw motion. "Impostor" feelings rise in a new situation, fall as the situation becomes familiar, and rise again in the next new circumstance. When Jeanne Stahl finished her studies of black, female college and high school students, she raised the point that IP feelings might become worse as someone moved out of a familiar role and into a new role that had yet to be mastered. I like to call this the "top dog" factor—leaving a comfortable position in which you have won some recognition and heading off into unfamiliar territory.

Ginger is an accountant, and she talked about how her belief that she was a fraud would ease just as she was coming to any "ending." "I knew I was finishing up and, suddenly, things shifted into perspective," she said. "I felt like I could see things clearly: that I had done okay, that it wasn't so hard, and I was good and I liked my work. Good, healthy feelings—*at the end*. It invariably happened at every ending: when I moved from a city, changed from school to career. Everything finally fit into place. There was always harmony.

"I saw things in perspective because I was leaving and it wouldn't last much longer—and I was going to something much harder, much worse. The whole machinery was going to start up again. And, suddenly, the familiar became so easy that I saw things realistically for the first time. I'm sure when I leave this job, it will become the most wonderful thing that ever happened, and I'll be brilliant at it."

The "endings" don't have to be major life changes. One woman told me how she would "milk" a project once it became familiar to her. She wanted to put off having to face the next new task.

Even when someone overcomes the feeling of being a fake, he may find it reappearing when he takes the *next* big step in his academic or professional career.

Perhaps the new role is actually that of becoming a success. Now in his late forties, Duane is a well-known actor living in Los Angeles. The confusion he experienced when he first became successful remained with him for many years.

As he spoke, Duane recalled an incident that he had never before connected with the fear of being exposed as an impostor. He had been asked to return to a regional theater where he had performed. But he offered an excuse, declining the invitation. "I see I must have been afraid I'd be found out, that they'd weary of me and not like me as much," he said.

Duane described the way he felt about becoming successful: "Finding out how people reacted to me was a surprise. I couldn't understand it. I never saw myself as that talented. Yet you're in show business because you think you have talent. That's the contradiction that goes with it. Why work at it? It's not as if I *had* to act. Without that feeling, I think I would have been *more* successful. I couldn't push my career or sell myself with any conviction because I didn't believe in myself."

In the early days of his career, said Duane, "I made more of a living than I had a right to. I did everything to keep myself from it. I didn't go to auditions; I hated the cattle call aspect of it, which is nonsense, because that's the name of the game. When I went, they liked me. After my success—I can't analyze my feelings. I was just always surprised. People were at my feet. Now I accept it, though it's still a surprise. I'm beginning to see the talent I have, the craft. I never understood the gift I had, the fact that I had it. If I had, I would have done much more."

THE JOB ITSELF

Every job or career has its own requirements, demands, and expectations for successfully playing the role. It may, for example, be perfectly acceptable for an art director in an advertising agency to come to work in jeans. Yet an account executive at that same agency might be expected to show up in a suit. In some companies, meetings are very relaxed, with lots of discussion and personal banter. In others, the atmosphere is much more formal. Either way, we find out what behavior is expected of us and adapt to our role.

For the person who is susceptible to the Impostor Phenomenon, certain types of jobs can actually cause feelings of fraudulence to become more intense. People who work independently and in creative fields are constantly faced by new projects. They can feel like their talents are repeatedly being tested. Their "impostor" feelings often grow worse if they believe every project is bringing them closer to being exposed as a fraud.

In some jobs and roles, the demands for success may require major changes in a person's attitudes or appearance.

Ted explains how, when he became an investment manager in Chicago, he felt that he was going to have to project a certain image if other people were going to trust him as an authority. He saw this image as integral to succeeding in his job. "I found that I couldn't attain what it was I wanted unless I acted as if I already had it," he said. "There was no way that somebody with five million dollars was going to give it to somebody who'd never seen five million dollars in his life."

Initially, Ted didn't try to save any of his earnings, but invested his money in such things as expensive suits and a new car—all designed to create an image of himself as the successful person he wanted to become. "I was very concerned with presenting myself as if I was at a level above where I currently was. It was sort of like a manifest destiny; it almost started to happen that way. I was aspiring to be successful and acting that way, faking it, being an impostor to success." Ted viewed this as "a sham, something I was putting over on people."

Now that he has achieved success, "I feel funny about the level of it," he said. "It's almost beyond my own realm of belief." Yet, "There's no way I can ever conceive of making less next year than I earned this year, and the following year I assume the same will be true. And I will aspire to that—acting 'as if,' as I'm already doing. Now it's easier because there's a sort of quantum area in there which I've overcome."

Ted recognizes his own skills and does feel entitled to the respect and admiration he gets from others. But he says he is quick to deflect compliments, quick to change the subject. He attributes part of the admiration he receives to the nature of his work. "There's an aura the business can create around an individual," he observed. "It's not unlike professional sports. The recognition is very high and the pressure is constant. It breeds individuals who become known in certain circles. I attribute it more to how the business sets you up."

The feeling of being a fake in his role as a successful investment manager remains with Ted still. "I'm aspiring to even higher levels, but I'm doing it, in my own opinion, by faking it to get there," was his comment. "I have the mind-set of a successful person, but I don't feel entitled to act that way. It's how I go through my day, working my ass off. I've got a goal out there that I have to aspire to, that I don't think I can really cut. I think I'm faking. Now I'm scared to death of failure and refuse to accept anything but success."

Other roles have more unusual requirements for success. They can lead to deep, long-lasting changes in outlook and personality traits. Most demanding are those roles where being successful can be a matter of life or death. In combat, for example, lives are at stake, and the consequences of a mistake or a failure are very different from those most of us encounter.

Hugh had become a platoon leader in Vietnam at the age of twenty-three. This position meant that he was required to spend a lot of time attending to details. Such detail-checking had survival value. Every night, for example, he would make sure that his men checked the pins in their grenades; men had blown themselves up by neglecting to do this.

In civilian life, Hugh carried over the habits that were adaptive in combat. Once he returned home, he became obsessed about considering every possible problem that might arise in a situation and always prepared for the worst. The same habits that had helped him in wartime led to a constant level of high anxiety that troubled him for years.

Buddy is a retired policeman now living in Florida. He explains that "being tough" is critical for a policeman if he is going to protect himself and do his job. "You have to put on this act that you're the tough guy," he said. "You can't back down. You can't run. If you go on a job and there's a man in an apartment with a gun, you *have* to be afraid—but you can't act that way."

He describes the approach as "a big bluff. You have to bluff the other guy. If you bluff him, you don't have the conflict. Once you have the conflict, there's nothing to say you're going to beat him, no matter what kind of facade you put up. The thing is to scare him down before he starts swinging. And the first time you find that your bluff worked, it gets bigger."

Even among other policemen, says Buddy, that "false front" has to be maintained to protect the tough image. And, he notes, the demands of this role are so extreme that it becomes impossible to turn it off: "The job does change the person. He gets to be closed. Cops tell no one their feelings, everything is held in. If you want to cry, you can't. You never see cops crying; they go into closets to cry, or they go into closets and blow their brains out."

"Once you get hard, the act is forever, always—on-duty, off-duty. You become this other person that you're really not. You don't realize you have this false front until you're not doing it anymore."

In his own career, said Buddy, "I knew I was a good cop, but I wasn't as tough as everyone thought I was. I guess my acting job or my impersonation of this tough cop convinced everyone that I was that tough." As he explained, whether out in the street or working with other policemen, the image must be flawless: "If you show your emotions, you'll give up your cover."

SOCIETY AND CULTURE

We know that both men and women can be victims of the Impostor Phenomenon. So it may surprise you to learn that this syndrome was first thought to be a problem mostly for women.

By going back to the beginning, when psychologists first started studying the Impostor Phenomenon, you can see why the syndrome was initially believed to be restricted to women. And that story leads into the way we learned about some of the other causes of the IP.

During the 1970s, Dr. Pauline Clance was practicing and teaching psychology at a Midwestern college. She began to notice that women students with a history of high academic achievement were expressing doubts about their intellectual abilities and competence.

These women had high scores on their college entrance examinations. Now they were receiving A's and favorable evaluations from their professors. Yet, they continued to worry that they had fooled others into believing they were more intelligent than they actually were. Several of them thought the college admissions committee had made an error in admitting them to the school, or that there was some mistake made when their college entrance exams had been scored.[2]

Clance, along with Dr. Suzanne Imes, began to study this phenomenon among a group of 150 highly successful women. These women were primarily white, middle to upper class, and between the ages of twenty and forty-five. A third of them were patients in the doctors' private practice; the other two-thirds were students in small seminar classes or workshops run by the two psychologists.

The women in this group were respected in their professions or had achieved academic excellence. They, too, expressed feelings that they were simply intellectual impostors, and feared that sooner or later they would be discovered as frauds by their bosses, professors, and peers.

In 1978, Clance and Imes wrote about the women they'd been studying.[3] They had some specific ideas about why this phenomenon was more of a problem for one sex than for the other.

As they noted, there has been a stereotype of women as being incompetent. And they proposed that women have mentally adopted this sex-role stereotype as being true; many women have internalized it as part of their own self-images.

Clance and Imes talked about previous work in psychology, which supported this theory. It made a strong case.

They mentioned the work of Kay Deaux, who in 1976 had reviewed all the research on the different ways men and women explain success and failure.[4] Deaux had concluded that men tend to *expect* to succeed and attribute success to enduring, stable, internal factors, such as ability. On the other hand, Deaux found, a great deal of research suggested that women typically *don't* expect to succeed. When they do, they attribute the cause of their success to temporary, unstable factors. They might attribute it to something external to themselves which they can't control—such as luck. Or, they might say it was the result of something internal, but *temporary,* such as effort.

When it comes to failure, said Deaux, men and women switch sides. Men typically see failure as the result of some factor *outside* themselves, like bad luck or the extreme difficulty of the task at hand. Women are more likely to assume the blame for failure, explaining it by something internal like lack of ability.

For women, this is the worst of all possible worlds. They feel that it's their own fault if they fail. But if they succeed, they don't take the credit. So it's easy to see why a woman might feel like she's not responsible for her success and must be a phony who's fooling other people.

WOMEN AND THE FEAR OF SUCCESS

I've talked about the ways in which the fear of success can lead someone to believe he is a fake. However, the fear of success doesn't always have to be based solely on someone's family background or individual personality. There are social and cultural factors that can also contribute to it.

The fear of success in women has been widely talked and written about, and deserves some special attention here. The idea of a highly successful woman goes against long-held social stereotypes. A woman who dares to achieve is breaking the rules—a frightening idea.

When Clance and Imes first wrote about the Impostor Phenomenon, they connected feelings of fraudulence specifically to women's fear of success. They cited Matina Horner's famous research on this subject. Dr. Horner's study had suggested that many women in our culture have an unconscious motive to avoid success: They fear that they will be penalized if they do succeed by being rejected or seen as unfeminine.[5]

Horner had done her work with a group of college students at the University of Michigan in the 1960s. She asked 90 women to write a story beginning with the line: "After first-term finals, Anne finds herself at the top of her medical school class." The idea behind this storytelling approach was that the students would identify with the fictitious "Anne." Without being aware of it, they would express how they felt about being successful themselves.

According to many of these students, "Anne" was going to have to pay dearly for her accomplishment in loneliness and rejection. Or else, she was going to come up with some reason to walk away from her success. Over 65 percent of the women predicted some negative consequence for the high-achieving "Anne." Their stories indicated that they saw success as something they should avoid.

Horner also gave this story-completion test to 88 male students from the school. But this time, it was "John" who made it to the top of his class. The men's stories didn't show this same fear of succeeding. Less than 10 percent thought that John would suffer negative consequences for his achievement.

Later on, this research was replicated, but this time both the "Anne" and "John" stories were given to men and women.[6] And the majority of *both sexes* suggested that "Anne" would be sorry for her success, while "John" would suffer far fewer penalties. These students perceived that "Anne" had violated the female sex-role stereotype by doing so well in medical school. So they expected that she would be punished in some way.

By believing that she is an impostor or intellectual phony, said Clance and Imes, the high-achieving woman can still live out her desire to achieve. But she avoids the negative consequences of success for women in our culture. In other words, if she thinks she is only an impostor, a woman can unconsciously deny her true competence in a "man's world" and avoid her fear of rejection. For some women, the Impostor Phenomenon may be the lesser of two evils. These psychologists also suggested that another motive women might have to deny their success is a fear of power.

As sexual stereotypes have weakened and women's roles have continued to expand in our society, I think we're already seeing this gender-related fear of success diminish. Young girls can now see that other women are succeeding without paying a penalty or being socially rejected. I hope they will learn that they can achieve, and still be accepted and loved, just as men can.

However, Clance and Imes originally felt the Impostor Phenomenon was found less frequently, and with less intensity, among men. They thought that the men who did suffer from the IP were primarily those who were more in touch with their "feminine" qualities. But they pointed out that more evidence was needed.

The idea that the Impostor Phenomenon was a woman's problem persisted. In 1982, Dr. Madeline Hirschfeld did her doctoral dissertation at Fordham University on the Impostor Phenomenon in successful career women.[7] She studied eighty women working in fields that had traditionally been associated with men, such as business, law, and engineering. Their ages ranged from twenty to sixty, and they were well-educated, with nearly 70 percent having pursued their education beyond the level of a bachelor's degree. The group's average annual salary was $38,000.

Hirschfeld gave these women several psychological scales to find out what factors might contribute to the IP. One scale, for example, tapped into their self-acceptance in career areas. Her results suggested that, like other IP victims, the women in the study who suffered from feelings of fraudulence didn't see ability as being the primary reason for their success. Further, these women didn't think they were properly prepared to be successful in their careers. They felt that their parents hadn't helped them acquire the traits needed for careers that weren't traditionally thought of as feminine.

Another possibility suggested by some early research was that minority women were especially prone to become IP victims. In 1980, Dr. Jeanne Stahl and her colleagues at Morris Brown College in Georgia had found strong "impostor" feelings among young black women. Over half (55 percent) of these women spoke of hard work, determination, and perseverance as the major causes of their success.

Dr. Stahl had performed an earlier pilot study of black, female students in their first year of college.[8] She found that *93 percent* of those college women attributed their success to characteristics other than intelligence. Why was this percentage so much higher than among the high school seniors she tested? After doing her two studies, Stahl raised the question of whether moving out of the "top" position (senior in high school) into a new "bottom" role (college freshman) might cause the feeling of being an impostor to grow stronger.

High achievers who are female *and* black represent a "double minority." If they are successful in a career, they may have violated social stereotypes for both their sex and their race. That immediately gives them two reasons to have trouble adjusting their self-images to their success. No one has yet tested women in any other racial or ethnic minority, but we can assume this would hold true for them as well.

The first clues that the IP wasn't only a woman's problem had appeared in 1979, when Suzanne Imes wrote her dissertation at Georgia State University.[9] She studied 80 female and 64 male faculty members from a large, urban university in the Southeastern United States. Imes wanted to see if there was a connection between feelings of fraudulence and how closely someone identified with his or her sex role. Would women scoring high on a Femininity scale be more likely to show that basic sign of the IP, attributing their success to something other than ability?

Imes looked at four categories: Femininity (high score on feminine sex role identification, low on masculine), Masculinity (high score on masculine identification, low on feminine), Androgynous (high on both feminine and masculine), and Undifferentiated (low on both feminine and masculine).

She also gave these faculty members a list of ten achievements common to people in their profession. They were asked to rate how much they saw different factors such as ability, luck, and likableness as contributing to their success in these ten areas.

As it turned out, Imes didn't find what she had expected. Sex or sex role differences apparently weren't connected to the feeling of being a fraud. The only people who stood out as high IP sufferers on the basis of sex roles were the "undifferentiated" group—those who didn't identify strongly with either masculine or feminine sex roles.

In 1980, I began studying the Impostor Phenomenon. I was fascinated by this syndrome. For one thing, I had experienced it myself in graduate school, so I knew what it meant to feel like a fraud. But I also thought about how the ideas behind the Impostor Phenomenon had been explored throughout the years in different fields. Psychologists, sociologists, and philosophers had all written about the themes of a public and private self, success-related guilt, and feelings of alienation connected to roles. Yet no one had connected them all with this one syndrome. I started by tying research from different fields together with the Impostor Phenomenon.[10]

At this point, I realized we needed an objective way to measure IP feelings. Different psychologists had to have a means of directly comparing their studies. I wanted to design something simple and efficient, so that it could be used in situations where time was limited.

Based on all the existing research, I devised a list of statements in the form of a psychological scale. Then I tested it until I was sure it was a valid means of measuring the IP. This list came to be the Harvey IP Scale.[11]

Once I had the scale, I was able to start investigating whether this syndrome was truly more of a problem for women and blacks. With the help of my colleagues, Louise Kidder and Lynn Sutherland, I studied 30 people working in a city as high school teachers, social workers, crisis counselors, and middle-management administrators in human services.[12] The group included both men and women, blacks and whites. All of them had obtained at least a bachelor's degree from college.

Consistent with previous ideas on the IP, I assumed we would find that women experienced feelings of fraudulence more than men, and blacks more than whites. Much to my surprise, I found there were no significant differences on either count. Even the "double minority" idea didn't hold up here: Black women had no higher degree of IP feelings than anyone else.

In 1981, I presented my findings that the Impostor Phenomenon affected men and women equally. More and more evidence was accumulating to show us that this was true. Dr. Gail Matthews, working with Pauline Clance, interviewed 41 men and women in different professions. They reported on their findings in 1984. Members of both sexes said they had experienced feelings of fraudulence, and there was no statistically significant difference in the number of men and women who'd had these feelings.

Dr. Margaret Gibbs and her colleagues had done a

study of psychotherapists and the IP, also in 1984. Again, there were no real differences between the percentages of men and women who reported impostor feelings.

When Michael Penland and Dr. Susan McCammon gave the Harvey IP Scale to 57 college freshmen and sophomores, they also found that people of either sex could be IP victims. In Dr. Mary Topping's study of nearly 300 university faculty members, the men actually had a *higher* group average on the Harvey IP Scale than did the women.

At the 1981 meeting of the American Psychological Association, I explained my theory that the Impostor Phenomenon was first discovered in women because they were more likely than men to be willing to talk about such feelings. As a group, women tend to be more attuned to their feelings in general and better able to disclose them to others. Men have often felt they must ignore or suppress their feelings in order to maintain the traditional masculine "strong, silent type" image. And during the 1970s, the women's movement had encouraged support groups and other opportunities for women to examine their feelings. Men didn't have these same opportunities.

When research on the Impostor Phenomenon was just getting underway, psychologists were working without an objective scale to measure "impostor" feelings in both sexes. We were spending more time *talking* with women about their feelings in open-ended discussions. Because women were more easily able to reveal their feelings of fraudulence, it appeared at first that the IP was a problem only, or mostly, for the female sex. But now we know that the IP can just as easily affect men. Men simply weren't talking about it.

This kind of turnaround in psychologists' thinking is actually an unusual one. In science, it is rare to find an issue identified in women first, later extended to include men. Historically, research has proceeded in the opposite direction—that is, focusing first on men, tending to overlook women.

Those of us who attend conferences where the Impostor Phenomenon is discussed have noticed something else. For several years, when papers on this syndrome were presented, the people who came to the meetings were almost all women. Recently, we see there are many more men in the audience, eager to talk about their personal experiences with this problem.

BEING "ONE OF A KIND"

Psychologists had seen that one's sex or race alone didn't make someone more likely to be an IP victim. But that still left us with unanswered questions. Why had so many black women in Stahl's studies assumed their achievements weren't based on intelligence? Were there other social or cultural factors that could bring on, or intensify, feelings of fraudulence?

At the time I did my study of a sample of 30 people in different professions, I had some other ideas brewing in mind. Could it be that IP feelings were increased simply by the realization that one is somehow *different* from one's peers?

Maybe, I thought, past research had been attributing IP feelings to race and sex differences when the issue was really that of simply *seeing oneself as unusual, or different from other people*. High-achieving women and blacks have often found themselves in work situations where they stand out as being "the only one" of their kind. Being female and being black might be just two of the ways in which IP victims could be atypical in relation to their peers.

THE ONLY MAN, THE ONLY WOMAN

To find out more about this idea, I asked these 30 people to tell me how typical they felt their career was for someone of their sex. Did they feel it was unusual for a person of their gender to work in their particular field?

I analyzed their answers and there it was. On the average, those who perceived their careers as atypical for someone of their sex had a significantly higher degree of "impostor" feelings than those who did not. *It made no difference whether they were male or female.* "Impostor" feelings were stronger in those women who felt they were in "male" professions. But they were also stronger in those men who felt they were in "female" professions.

These results hearkened back to work done by psychologists Frances Cherry and Kay Deaux in 1975.[13] They had found that *both* men and women may wish to avoid possible penalties for violating sex role stereotypes in our culture.

Of course, there was a time when *most* professions were considered "male"—particularly those that involved having authority over other people. Women, it was thought, weren't supposed to work unless they had to. Old attitudes die hard and we can imagine that the fear of violating a sex role stereotype still poses a problem for great numbers of women.

In the same way, a man might prefer to deny his natural capabilities for a traditionally "female" career. He doesn't want to be thought of as unmasculine. There are fewer jobs where men might have to deal with this dilemma, but many fields that employ men are traditionally associated with women. They range from social work, teaching, and nursing to working in a day care center, from airline attendant to telephone operator. Although times are changing, some people still hold on to the stereotype that says there is something suspect about a man who chooses to do a "woman's job."

As it is for the person who fears success, the Impostor Phenomenon can be an unconscious form of psychological protection for someone whose job is atypical for his or her sex. He is afraid of the penalties that might result from having violated his sex role stereotype. The penalties could be suspicion by others of one's femininity or masculinity or, worse, complete social rejection. By thinking of himself as an impostor, this person can mentally defend himself against these possible penalties. *He doesn't connect himself with his success.* He isn't aware of why he is thinking of himself in this way, but his unconscious mind is helping him to get around his fears.

If someone believes he is an impostor, he has found a way of saying to himself that he isn't *really* good at what he does; he is simply giving the impression that he's good at it, or "playacting," even though the evidence may say otherwise. If he thinks he's untalented or incompetent, he doesn't have to admit to himself that he's suited to a career that isn't socially acceptable or "right" for someone of his sex. Without realizing it, he's fighting off the frightening idea of being punished for "stepping out of line."

There are other ways besides gender in which you can be atypical or unique in your job. It might be your racial or ethnic background. If you are black, Oriental, Chicano, or Hispanic, and you work mostly among Caucasians, you have another area in which you "stand out" as being different from your peers. A recent newspaper article quoted a column written by a young black woman, a senior at a predominantly white university; she had spoken about "four long years of feeling like a speck of pepper mistakenly dropped into the salt bin."[14]

Many forms of "uniqueness" can contribute to feelings of fraudulence. When someone observes that he or she is the only one of a certain type of person in a role, he might easily (though wrongly) conclude that he doesn't belong in that role. The high-school students in Dr. Stahl's study suffered from "uniqueness" on three counts: They were black, they were women, and they planned to enter traditionally male school majors of science and engineering.

Some research has suggested that whatever features make people *different* from their peers tend to be more important to their sense of identity than the features they have *in common* with their peers.[15] In other words, people are more highly aware of what sets them apart, or makes them unique, than what makes them the same as others. It might be their sex, race, ethnic background, nationality, or social class. When they define their own identities, they often give disproportionate weight to these unique qualities.

On the job, then, a man among women, or a non-white among whites, may pay a great deal of attention to the feature that sets him apart. This person might disregard what he has in common with his peers—his abilities and qualifications. Therefore, he can decide he doesn't fit in, doesn't belong.

Some studies have shown that women receive even more credit than men when they act competently in traditionally male areas of achievement. This means that when someone displays an unexpected level of competence, the achievement is magnified. This is known as the "talking platypus phenomenon."[16] (You wouldn't think anything of it if you saw a platypus sitting out in the sun. But you'd be pretty impressed if he looked up at you and remarked, "Nice day if it don't rain.")

I remember riding to the airport one day on a bus being driven by a woman. Once we got to the terminal, she began moving the suitcases out of the luggage compartment. As they observed her carrying these heavy bags, several of the passengers commented, "Isn't she wonderful? Isn't she terrific?" This woman was acting at the same level of competence as a man would in this job, but more competently than some of the passengers expected of a woman. She got more credit for her actions than a man would have by doing the identical thing.

Similarly, a black who is unique among whites in a given situation may be described as "a credit to his race." This is never said about whites—only about blacks and other racial minorities.

Interestingly, this idea contradicts the notion that women and minorities have to do *twice* as good a job as their white male counterparts to get any recognition. It all works to add to the confusion and insecurity that may arise in someone about whether he truly "belongs."

TOKENISM

People who are different from their peers because of their gender or race may have to struggle with their fears of violating a sexual or racial stereotype. But they may face another troubling idea as well. This is the notion that they have been chosen for their position simply as a "token."

If someone stands out because of his sex, race, or nationality, he can begin to question whether the quality that makes him different is *actually the reason he has gotten ahead.* A woman may wonder if she is being channeled into a management position because "they need a woman in that job right now." A black student admitted to a college or graduate program may wonder what would have happened if the admissions committee hadn't known he was black.

Although she was trained as a nurse, thirty-eight-year-old Adrienne spent five years working for a Connecticut food corporation, which had few women in the management ranks. She started at the bottom, delivering the company's products, and "in the beginning, I felt great and I enjoyed it," she said. "I had just moved to the area and needed a job, and I felt it was time for me to do something different. Out there with the boys, I had the strength and stamina of a twenty-year-old."

Adrienne was promoted every year for three years in a row. She knew she had always received good evaluations but was feeling that these levels of corporate management weren't "true" to her. When the next promotion came, she began to doubt seriously whether she should have taken it. It seemed to her she had been a lot happier in the days when she was making deliveries on the road. She also felt the company had her "tracked as a woman who was capable of doing the job and they needed a woman up there in the ranks."

Adrienne said she needed to prove to herself and to the world at large that she wasn't going to be stuck in the female role, and this was part of her motivation for staying in a traditionally male job. The higher salary, too, had "ensnared" her, she said.

Her confusion about this situation was causing Adrienne great unhappiness and she was feeling like a fraud in her higher-level job. She also believed she wasn't meeting her own standards. "Over the past year, I've been skirting and faking and pretending, but still getting good evaluations from the bosses," she related. "I would think, 'What a bunch of morons—how can they be giving me good evaluations?' I know I haven't been doing a good job. There are certain commitments you have to meet, and I've been meeting them only minimally."

When she started moving up the corporate ladder, Adrienne felt it was a challenge. Soon she had surpassed her brother and sister in salary level. It seemed almost too easy to her. And, she said, "It got to be very heady to be pulling in a sizable salary. It never created any anxiety for me until this past year, when I've been feeling guilty about not doing a good enough job."

Adrienne was troubled by the distance her promotions had put between her and her original co-workers. "When I got my first promotion into the supervisory lower echelons of management, I still had a feeling of being buddies with my co-workers," she said. "There were no women, but I still had a camaraderie with the guys. As soon as I moved up the next notch, leaving them there, I became conscious of almost instant alienation and separation. Some of them were there ten or twelve years, and I was there two. Maybe it was me, but it felt like they were thinking, 'We helped to train her and then we brought her up to this level, and now she's going to be above us.' "

Adrienne was questioning her work from every perspective. "There are some instances of deception that I think are necessary in the corporate world. And so, I'd try to play their games, and then I'd start fudging in order to continue to play games. And that would create anxiety in me for not being true to my own sense of idealism. In the last three or four years, I've felt that I've been functioning on a level that wasn't the real me.

"Sometimes I wonder if this is a midlife crisis. Most

men just stick with it. An isolated few get out of the rat race and do something else. But most don't. I guess I allow myself to consider choices they don't even know are there."

Adrienne was torn over whether to continue her climb up through management or look at some other options. She felt she would have to make a break and pursue a different career, perhaps in social services. She was well aware that this would mean a lower salary. Yet, she commented, "I think women see below the surface. Men have heart attacks and become alcoholics, which is a path I easily could take if I keep on."

The quality that makes one different doesn't have to be as physically obvious as sex or skin color. An Englishman, for example, might find that Americans react positively to his English accent. He may wonder if it's really his accent, not him, who's been getting all those dinner party invitations. At work, he might suspect his American boss is impressed with him simply because the boss likes the way he speaks. Perhaps, he thinks, this employer believes anything said with a British accent sounds intelligent and sophisticated.

I believe quotas and affirmative action programs are necessary to correct past discrimination against disadvantaged groups. However, when they are put into practice, they may lead some high achievers to doubt the validity of their successes, particularly if they are already susceptible to the Impostor Phenomenon. Once on the job, such a person may have to deal with *other people's* suspicion that he is unqualified, only there because of some policy. It takes a great deal of self-confidence to hold onto one's self-image as bright and capable when others continually question it. If his colleagues act coolly toward him, or are skeptical about whether he can handle the work, this person can begin to question his own abilities. He may be psychologically worn down by the subtle—or not-so-subtle—doubts or hostility expressed by other people.

One female executive offered this thought: "I think as a woman you start off at a disadvantage. If a man walks into a meeting with a suit on, the immediate assumption is, 'He's smart,' until he proves otherwise. Whereas, when a woman walks into a meeting and she's pretty, the immediate assumption is, 'Gee, she must be nice.' You have to prove you're smart. So you sort of start off behind the eight-ball."

Even if other people don't present any problems in the situation, feeling that one is a "token" can still bring on great confusion and uncertainty about the cause of one's accomplishments. The IP victim looks at what makes him different from others and interprets it as evidence that he doesn't belong. Therefore, he reasons, he must have arrived at his position through fraudulent means. He may mistakenly attribute his accomplishments to this "tokenism" and feel that he is an impostor who hasn't truly earned his success.

THE FIRST-GENERATION PROFESSIONAL

Some people are "one of a kind" in a completely different way. They stand out from their own *families* because of their level of education. So I asked the people in my study how typical their educational level was in relation to their family background.

Their answers told me that this was another important issue for IP victims. The average IP score was higher among those who reported *reaching an educational level unusually high in relation to their family background*. Those who scored low on the IP Scale reported that their educational level was much more consistent with that of their relatives. And this was true regardless of whether they were male or female, black or white.

This suggested that "impostor" feelings are often connected *with feelings about changing one's social class*. Researchers had found strong feelings of fraudulence among high-achieving blacks. But it looked like the fact that they were black wasn't the most important point. It could simply have been a case of people—regardless of their race—trying to cope with the idea of a new social status.

As the number of women and minorities has increased in the professions, more of them are being faced with the problem of adjusting to a different social status. Anyone from a working-class or poor background who has changed his or her social status is in the same situation.

Making this kind of adjustment can be a problem for members of any race or ethnic background and either sex. People may wonder if they really belong in their new social class and this idea can lead to feelings of phoniness. Under these circumstances, blacks, whites, Hispanics—anybody—can have mixed feelings about their success. (You might remember from my own story that I was the first one in my family to earn a college degree.)

The person who works his way up to a social status that is higher than his family's is a "first-generation professional." He is the first one among his relatives to reach a particular level of achievement. Through education or special training, he is in a career that is better-paying or more prestigious than those of his family members. Perhaps his relatives have always done some kind of manual labor, and he is the first to work in a white-collar job. This person may make more money than anyone else in his family, and travel in different professional and social circles.

Though some people haven't gone to college or graduate school, they still may have moved into jobs that are quite different and more prestigious than those of their families. Even though my study only asked about the level of education, it suggested that these other types of first-generation professionals could also be more prone to IP feelings. I've found that this is so through my own conversations with people suffering from the Impostor Phenomenon.

Adam had been told since childhood that he embodied the hopes of his working-class Detroit family, and they saw a college education as a means of social mobility. But once he had entered college, his family appeared to withdraw from him, making him feel as if he no longer belonged. If he disagreed with them on any issue, he was criticized for "having an attitude." Their message was that he was becoming arrogant, acting as if he were too good for them.

Adam began to change his attitudes in a chameleonlike way to fit in with whatever group he was with—his family, old friends, college peers. But his method of adapting to the situation made him feel fraudulent. His "impostor" feelings and behavior persisted into his adult professional life. He also became overly modest in his behavior and was unable to accept any compliments on his successes. He was afraid he would be thought of as arrogant and others would then reject him.

There are many reasons why first-generation professionals might feel like impostors. They are well aware that their backgrounds are different from those of their new peers, so they may be unsure about whether they really "belong." Women or members of a minority group can also wonder if they are getting ahead simply because they're "tokens."

Their achievements often place them out in front as "representatives-at-large" for their families and/or communities. Therefore, they imagine disastrous and shameful consequences if they should fail. They feel they must be perfect—but, of course, no one can live up to that standard.

At the same time they are afraid of failing, they can also be afraid of what will happen if they should succeed. Will they become outsiders to their families and old friends? They may also feel guilty about surpassing the achievements of others in their families. Unconsciously, they might downplay or deny their successes by explaining them as fake or fraudulent.

Here is how the picture might be broken down:

TRAVELING IN UNCHARTED WATERS

The first-generation professional is venturing into unfamiliar territory. No one in his family has been through the same experiences he is now going through. So he can't turn to his relatives for advice and guidance on how to handle his new role.

This individual must try to fit in with his new peers at school or at work. Often, he feels socially and intellectually unprepared. His new peers may chat offhandedly about their sailing weekends or the year they studied in Europe. He never had an opportunity to experience these things, but he doesn't want to be humiliated by revealing that fact.

College students who come from working-class or poor backgrounds can worry about whether they really belong among the other students from more privileged backgrounds. A young man or woman from a working-class background who is starting an important new job might also feel out of place among his or her colleagues. This person may imagine that his co-workers all come from families long associated with the world of big business, that they already know exactly how to behave and what to do in their roles.

Back at home, the first-generation professional often has to cope with other difficulties. His family may not understand what his new world is like. It can be hard for him to communicate to them about his experiences and problems. One college freshman, the first in his family to go beyond high school, told me his parents envisioned college as something from a 1920s movie: nothing but cars, girls, and fun.

This type of person may also be afraid that he will become an "outsider" to his own family. He worries that if he changes too much, he will no longer fit in with his family, not to mention his old friends. In addition, though many working-class families are proud of their children's accomplishments, some can send mixed messages to their high-achieving child. Adam, for example, had to face his family's criticism, namely, that he considered himself too good for them now.

Brian was from a family of farmers in Kansas and spoke to me about his days on the track team in high school. He remembered feeling the exhilaration of being "out in front" and then, suddenly, being struck by a fear he didn't understand. So he "dropped back with the pack" where it was "safe."

As an adult, Brian was unconsciously afraid to succeed. He feared that success would set him apart from his family. He also worried that others would envy or resent him, talk about him behind his back, or try to retaliate against him. As a result, he avoided any situations that involved competition, or those where he was likely to stand out in any way. Whenever he undertook a major new project that might lead to some success, he hid it from his family until after it was well underway.

Brian based his self-image on the view that others held of him. He realized that success might bring him

221

praise and admiration from his family and old friends, and this was certainly desirable to him. But he also felt that any failure would bring shame too terrible to be endured. So each achievement became magnified in his mind as a crucial event.

Even worse, the first-generation professional may feel like an outsider in *both* his old world and his new one. On the one side, there is his family and community; on the other, his new social environment. Torn between the two, he may not completely identify with either. Although he may play the various roles associated with his new social status, it takes time to assimilate these roles into his self-concept. In the meantime, he feels like he doesn't belong anyplace.

For some first-generation professionals, performing competently becomes a role that must be played as if it were taking place on a stage. Lionel was a young man who was doing very well in his career and he was the first in his family to reach the management level in business. Each time he was promoted, the feeling that he was a fraud would resurface. As he put it: "In every new position I've ever held, I always feel additional pressure to do well, like it's my test . . . I'm on stage, and everyone will know if I don't do well."

THE STANDARD BEARER

Being bright and talented, a first-generation professional is often designated as the "standard bearer" for his family. Everyone at home is looking to him to bring honor to the family name and "do them proud." This can put the individual under a great deal of pressure. He may no longer see his successes or failures as his own. Instead, they are now events that can bring honor or shame to his entire family.

Some people are designated as the standard bearers for more than just their families. They must represent their entire community. Perhaps this high achiever comes from a small, tightly knit community; everyone in the community has known him since he was a child, and shares the family's pride in his achievements.

The burden of being a standard bearer can be of particular concern to minority group members. William Banks, a psychologist and professor of Afro-American studies at the University of California at Berkeley, studied the problems of black professors.[17] After sending out questionnaires to 192 black academicians and interviewing 26 of them, he found that they faced pressure from several fronts. The black students expect them to be mentors and role models; the university administrators want them to act as liaisons between the black students and community; and the black community sees them as representatives. Banks also found that some black professors, particularly females, have to contend with feeling socially isolated when there are few other black colleagues at the school.

As "representatives-at-large" for their families or communities, first-generation professionals may be plagued with more anxieties about failure and success than others who don't face such social pressures. They carry a heavy burden. They now feel they must be perfect not only to advance themselves, but also to reflect well on the people depending on them back home. This can lead them to see any mistake they make as a fatal flaw, with disastrous consequences for everyone involved.

For anyone who suffers from severe "impostor" feelings, a mistake is devastating. But the IP victim who is a standard bearer has further reason to dread the idea of failing or making some error. He thinks his performance must be perfect to avoid disappointing or bringing shame upon others. Once he has become successful, he feels an even greater pressure to maintain that success.

Because he wants to appear flawless in his work, he can't let anyone know of his fears, struggles, and disappointments. He believes he must maintain a perfect image of himself for the sake of others and so he can go on being accepted. That means he deprives himself of any possible support. Sometimes, the person in this position has yet another psychological burden to carry. He can begin to feel he is valued only for his performance in one role, not for himself as a whole, complex human being.

Dennis was a first-year student in a California business school. He had become consumed by the fear that he would fail, and said he was "obsessed and crazy" before every exam. He was unable to sleep before his tests and constantly visualized how humiliating failure would be for him.

Dennis had always been "the smart one" in his family, the one his mother and father could brag about to friends and relatives. The family had enough money to be considered well-off, with a nice house in the suburbs and a new car every year. Yet Dennis was the first among his relatives to attend college.

Throughout high school and college, he had been preparing for exams by obsessively memorizing every detail about the subject at hand. At times, he experienced a writing block that gave him trouble with his papers. He would procrastinate and worry, but finally manage to get the job done.

Dennis had a younger brother who caused a great deal of trouble for the family. His brother did poorly in school and traveled with the wrong crowd, managing to get into all kinds of scrapes. Dennis often felt he was compensating to their parents for his brother's deficiencies. Even so, he sensed that his brother, with all his problems, was loved and accepted by the family for who he was. Dennis doubted whether the same was true for him. His feelings of being valued and accepted had become hopelessly entangled with the role that he played in the family of high achiever and standard bearer.

After college, Dennis took a job managing a restaurant. At first he worried constantly that he wasn't doing a good job. Eventually, though, he began to feel more competent, and saw that his boss was pleased with his work. Things were going well all around; he was also enjoying his relationship with his long-time girlfriend, who had grown up right near him and never gone away to college. He felt that he might get married and settle into "the simple life." He would work and provide for the family, while his wife would stay at home and raise the children.

At the same time, though, Dennis couldn't keep from fantasizing about what he called "life in the fast track." His parents encouraged him to apply to business school and pursue a more prestigious, higher-paying job. Dennis hadn't really thought about how he would like business school or the type of job that might follow, but he viewed this move as "the thing to do." A degree from business school was a high-status achievement for someone from his family background.

Once he got to graduate school, Dennis found that his old study habits of memorizing everything weren't going to work anymore. There was simply an overwhelming amount of material and the time limits on exams wouldn't permit him to write it all down, even if he could have memorized it. Still, he clung to his old habits and became exceedingly anxious when he thought about giving them up. They were like a security blanket to him even though they were no longer useful.

All Dennis's fears and anxieties came together during the month he waited for the results of his midterm exams. He was convinced he had failed, and became totally preoccupied with trying to decide what direction his life should take. He realized he felt like an impostor in business school, because, instead of following his own desires, he was fulfilling his parents' wishes to share his status vicariously. The fact that he had made friends at school and enjoyed socializing with them also made him fear he would lose "the simple life" with his girlfriend. He was afraid of having failed his exams because he and his family would both be humiliated; yet if he succeeded in business school, he anticipated tremendous pressures to continue, possibly having to change his life dramatically, even if it wasn't what he really wanted to do. He felt he would be obligated to fulfill his potential.

Dennis's fear of flunking out was masking an unconscious wish to fail. If he did flunk his exams, he felt his major life decisions would be made for him. When he envisioned seeing the posted grades with F's next to his name, he experienced deep humiliation, but also a sense of relief. He would be free to escape to his "simple life" instead of pursuing a high-status education for his family's sake. He would also find out, once and for all, if he was truly loved and accepted by his parents for himself alone, or only for his performance and the honor his achievements could bring to the family.

Dennis wanted to continue as an "impostor" to preserve his family's image of him as brilliant, flawless, and problem-free; but he also wanted to be free of the pressure of having to do so. He couldn't take the responsibility for revealing himself, so he feared—and secretly hoped—that failed exams would do it for him.

In fact, he didn't have to fail his exams to stop living out the role that wasn't right for him. He could have gone back to his old job or taken a leave of absence from school until he decided what he wanted to do. Instead, he remained caught in a conflict between a fear of failure and a fear of success brought on by his role as the family standard bearer.

Throwing Away the Mask

SEVEN

In the course of reading this book, you may have come to realize that you've been suffering from the Impostor Phenomenon without knowing what it was. Now that you've looked at different areas of your life, you may be saying to yourself, "Yes, *that's* why I've been so anxious and afraid. I think people will find out I'm not good enough, or smart enough." Perhaps you've known for years that you felt like an impostor—but never realized this feeling had a name, or that it's shared by so many other people.

Okay, you know you've got these "impostor" feelings. Now you want to know what you can do about it. In this chapter, you will find some answers. There are a number of ways to peel away the impostor "mask" and free yourself of the IP.

The Impostor Phenomenon affects you in three different areas: your thoughts, your feelings, and your behavior. It must be attacked on all three fronts. These three areas are interrelated—what affects one affects the others—so it hardly matters where you begin. Keep in mind, however, that your feelings, your emotions, are the most resistant to change, and that barrier will probably be the last to fall. Don't be discouraged if you change the way you think and act, but find that your old IP feelings still bother you at times.

Remember not to succumb to "all or none" thinking in setting your goal of defeating this syndrome. The Impostor Phenomenon is tenacious. Give yourself some credit for the degree of your improvement. You haven't failed if you don't completely banish your "impostor" feelings forever.

Curiously, not everyone *wants* to break free of the Impostor Phenomenon. Some people are afraid to let go of the belief that they are fakes. They see their fear of failure working as a sort of fuel to drive them on. It seems to them that the sense of being an impostor is motivating them to do a better job. They're afraid that if they weren't always worrying about being exposed as frauds, they would get "fat and lazy," and stop trying to excel.

One corporate executive commented that he doesn't want to get over his "impostor" feelings because he is afraid of becoming conceited and swellheaded. He dreaded the idea of acting like those executives who wouldn't give him "the time of day" when he first started out in his company. He described his fear of failure as "very positive, and I don't want it to stop. It's a fear I can deal with, and I can live with it." However, he pointed out, "It's not too good for your physical health. I work out as much as I can. I'm very aware of what it does to me mentally. It fries my mind."

The Impostor Phenomenon may motivate some. But for most IP victims, I've found that the pain and fear that go along with feeling like a fake are an unnecessary price to pay for success. I would say that believing you won't excel or achieve anymore if you stop feeling like an impostor is actually a form of magical thinking on a bigger scale. It's based on the fear of abandoning a ritual because you imagine that what you think will alter reality.

Consider whether the Impostor Phenomenon is

making you feel anxious and stressed. It's likely to be interfering with your enjoyment of your achievements and the rewards they bring. Would you like to see if you could be just as successful without operating on the adrenaline of fear? Do you wonder if you could be *more* successful than you are if you didn't feel that you are a fake? Maybe you feel the quality of your life and your relationships would improve if you could break loose from the IP.

Through my experience in treating people who suffer from the Impostor Phenomenon, I've developed certain methods that you can use to fight the feeling of being a fake. They are based on many different existing theories of helping people overcome certain psychological problems. Several psychologists, including Pauline Clance, Suzanne Imes, Gail Matthews, and myself, have adapted and written about various techniques in working with IP victims. I will offer you the strategies that I have used with people and that I believe are most helpful.

Keep in mind, however, that your feeling of being an impostor won't disappear overnight, no matter what you do. It can run very deep, and be firmly rooted in your image of yourself.

1. NAMING IT

Just by reading this book, you've already taken the first step toward loosening the IP's powerful grip. Now you know that you aren't alone, and that feelings of fraudulence are a problem for many people who are just like you. In fact, you can see that they're a problem for people who are even more successful than you are—people who might always seem to be totally self-assured and confident of themselves.

I've spoken with many IP victims who have expressed a tremendous sense of relief over finding out that the IP is a common problem and being able to give it a name. As one woman said to me: "I was so relieved to find out that other people had this. For years, I thought I was the only one who felt this way."

After an article appeared in *The New York Times* describing my work on the Impostor Phenomenon, I received a great number of phone calls and letters from people who had long suffered from the IP without knowing what it was. They talked about how comforting it was to see their own feelings described in the article.

One woman wrote to me: "I felt much as a gambler or foodaholic must feel when he learns for the first time that other people have the same problem and that it really is an illness of sorts. . . . Actually I spend a lot of time trying to find out whether people whom I consider to be successful feel the same way. Sometimes I am disappointed; they have the nerve to *feel* successful. At other times I am rewarded: they whisper over the lunch table, 'Do you feel that way too?' "

Now you recognize "the terrible secret" for what it is: a syndrome that is shared by many other people.

2. DAY-TO-DAY SOLUTIONS

Here are four steps you can follow to help you on a daily basis:

A. *Make a list of the times that "impostor" feelings are likely to strike.*

You probably know which situations intensify your own feeling of fraudulence. So take the step of *primary prevention*. Instead of trying to remedy the problem only after it's already happened, anticipate and plan for it ahead of time.

Write down the times when the feeling of being a phony flares up in full force. Is it when you take on a new assignment? When you have to make an important presentation at the office? When you give a large party? Consult this list weekly or monthly. This way you will recognize what you are experiencing the next time a similar event rolls around. That feeling of faking it shouldn't take you by surprise and throw you off-balance.

When you have identified the circumstances that have brought on IP feelings in the past, you can be ready for those feelings the next time. When you warn yourself to expect IP feelings, you're that much closer to keeping them from overwhelming you.

Prepare yourself for "impostor" feelings when you face important performance events. Sometimes you can tie your anxieties to a particular task that suddenly arises. You're told to attend a meeting with a potential new client. Or you're handed an application form for a new job or a grant. Maybe you're concerned with making a good impression at a specific social event. Friends call to say they're in the neighborhood and want to "drop in," but you haven't dusted or vacuumed. Or a man you're interested in calls, inviting you to a movie that starts in ten minutes; you haven't washed your hair and you suddenly notice a pimple on your chin. Any one of these situations could be the cause of a sudden IP attack.

Maybe your feelings of fraudulence have been more intense lately, and you can't figure out why. Think about what you've been doing in the past few weeks or months. Have you had a string of important projects at work that were especially challenging? Have you been coping with a crisis involving your parent, child, or friend? What you experience as a general feeling of fraudulence may actually be connected to a series of specific identifiable events.

You also know that people are more vulnerable to the IP in certain kinds of situations: for example, moving into a new role. Being promoted, switching to a new company, getting married, and having a baby all involve taking on a new role. Let's say you're starting in your first job, or you're suddenly making much more money than you did in the past. Perhaps you're moving into a position that is unusual for someone of your sex, age, or background. Or you're creating your own job and don't have anyone to whom you must answer. Are you a new CEO, or just opening up your own practice in law, medicine, or accounting?

Are you getting some public recognition for your work, talent, or philanthropy? This role is "new" in that you may not be used to receiving public attention. The scrutiny of others as you stand in the limelight may bring on the fear of being exposed as unworthy of the honor. Maybe you're in a job where you just don't get much feedback, so it seems to you that with every project you're starting from scratch.

Should you recognize IP feelings emerging, remind yourself that it's the newness of your role that is causing them. Don't interpret your sense of phoniness to mean that you're unqualified for the job, or not capable enough to handle it. You haven't yet learned all the ins and outs of your role; that doesn't mean you won't learn what you need to.

"Impostor" feelings don't mean you can't succeed. Sure, it would be nice to be able to play a role perfectly from day one. But that isn't how it works. So don't berate yourself for not being an expert at something you've never done before. Remember, you're not unqualified—you're only in the process of learning.

*   *   *

B. *When the feeling of being a fake starts to take hold, immediately remind yourself that this is a symptom of the Impostor Phenomenon, and not an objective truth.*

Once you can identify your feelings of phoniness as symptoms of the IP, you can start to do something about them. If you have objective evidence of success in what you're doing, you can see that your feelings are probably part of the IP syndrome. Accept, once and for all, that you aren't a fraud, but simply someone who *feels like* a fraud.

If, for example, you are about to make a presentation in a meeting, mentally review what you have done to prepare. Do you know what points you want to get across? Have you looked up your facts? Once you acknowledge that you have indeed done what was reasonably required to prepare, you'll see that your feelings are based on unrealistic fears instead of on reality.

If you experience the IP in an interpersonal relationship, ask yourself if your expectations of your role are realistic. Are they based on what others really require of you, or on your own unrealistic requirements of yourself? Are you telling yourself you're a fraud because you're an ordinary person, instead of someone ideal and special? Do you feel you must be better than others?

C. *Try to relax.*

This might sound to you like pretty basic advice, but it's very important. The feeling of being a fake can bring on intense anxiety. But you can't deal with that feeling when anxiety has you all wound up and frantic. You need to relax.

There are many relaxation techniques. Find one you like and use it whenever IP feelings strike. On a regular basis, you could do yoga, transcendental meditation, or self-hypnosis. Some people find that sports help them ease their tension; maybe you get some relief from a swim or a good game of tennis or squash. You might want to buy an audiotape program of exercises specifically designed to help you relax.

In addition I can recommend Edmund Jacobson's active progressive relaxation exercises, described in his book *Anxiety and Tension Control* (Boston: J. B. Lippincott, 1964). One set of these exercises involves alternately tensing and then relaxing muscle groups, starting with the feet and legs, and working up to the face and head. Another reference for relaxation exercises is *The Relaxation Response* by Herbert Benson (New York: Avon Books, 1976).

If you don't have time to do a full exercise or if "impostor" feelings hit suddenly, try some deep breathing to relieve tension. Inhale deeply and exhale very slowly until all the air is expelled from your lungs. Repeat this twice more. (Stop after three deep breaths, to avoid becoming dizzy or hyperventilating.)

Another relaxation method is visualization. Let your mind wander to a peaceful and relaxing scene, such as a warm beach, or a quiet forest—any place in which you can remember feeling serene. Imagine yourself in the scene, feeling relaxed and peaceful.

It doesn't matter what technique you choose. The important thing is to find a way to calm yourself.

D. *Isolate the task that is making you anxious and break it down into parts.*

Once you are calm and relaxed, consider the task at hand. It may seem like a big nightmare to you, but if you think about it, you can probably break it down into manageable parts.

If, for example, you have to give a presentation for a

new client, you have one project made up of several parts. You must decide what you want to say, organize your thoughts, write them down, and maybe even rehearse aloud.

Take these steps one at a time. Don't let them crowd your mind all at once. When you're thinking about what you're going to say, don't worry about how this or that thought will sound when you say it out loud. You'll work that out when you get to that point. And try not to let the other details surrounding this event get in your way. When you sit down to make your notes, don't distract yourself by wondering what you should wear on the big day or whether your car will be out of the garage by then so you can be sure to arrive on time.

If the task is a dinner party, don't try to handle everything at once, rushing back and forth from the kitchen to the dining room to the living room. Plan what needs to be done and leave yourself reasonable time to do it. Don't expect perfection. Others will not be expecting it of you. Remember that people come to enjoy your company. If they are only interested in food or ambience, they can go to a restaurant (and if they're only looking for a free meal, it doesn't matter what you serve or how the house looks).

Whenever possible, start with the *easiest* part of your task first. You know what aspects make you the least and most anxious. By starting out with the things you find easiest, you can see yourself accomplishing something, and you will feel more in control.

In the course of her job, Marie regularly had to write reports. She always attacked the most difficult part of the report first. This was her way of confronting her worst fear: the part of the report that she felt would ultimately expose her as a fraud. But this habit didn't help her. It only increased her anxiety to such a high level that she wasn't able to concentrate enough to accomplish anything for several days. So, in addition, she became afraid she wouldn't get the job finished on time—which made her even more anxious.

I suggested to Marie that she begin with the easiest parts instead. When she changed her pattern, she began to feel much better, much more in control. She was able to make some headway on the report quickly, which gave her a feeling of competence. And seeing some of the work actually done made her less fearful about not meeting her deadline.

When you face a performance event that elicits your IP feelings, make a list of what you have to do, starting with the things that are easiest for you. Gradually work your way down the list toward the more difficult parts. Let each step build upon the success of the previous one.

3. BEING HONEST AND OPEN

The fear of exposure brings with it a feeling of anxiety. One way to fight that anxiety is to be honest and open from the beginning about what you think, and about the things you don't know.

At first, this suggestion might seem bizarre, or, at the very least, impossible to follow. You're certainly not about to start telling people you think you're an impostor and therefore shouldn't be allowed to do what they're asking—or paying—you to do.

I'm *not* suggesting you do that. But the Impostor Phenomenon derives a great deal of its power from its secret nature and the fear that any flaw will reveal one as a fraud. Try to avoid falling into the trap of attempting to appear perfect, hiding any sign of nervousness, or concealing your lack of knowledge about something. That also goes for pretending to agree with someone else's opinions, interests, or approaches to plans or problems. For example, there's nothing shameful about a lawyer who can't immediately recall every detail of a past case that pertains to something he's working on. And it's not a mark of ignorance if you haven't read the new book being discussed at a cocktail party.

If you don't know something that you feel others expect you to know, don't keep silent or pretend that you do know. Your IP feelings will only get worse if you keep letting other people assume you understand exactly what they mean or what they're talking about when you really don't. If you've never ridden a horse or played tennis, don't imply that you have; you'll find yourself backed into a corner when the person you're talking with invites you to go riding or participate in a tennis weekend.

Don't be afraid to ask questions. When you're used to thinking that any question reveals you as ignorant, I know this is not an easy thing to do. But there's nothing wrong with saying, "I'm not quite sure what you mean" or "I'm not very familiar with that. Could you fill me in?" When your co-worker refers to an industry survey, you might ask, "Could you refresh my memory a bit on that?" If you've just received a new assignment or begun working with a client, you might say, "Let's go over it again so I'm sure I can give you exactly what you need."

If you're signing a financial agreement or a business deal, ask all the questions you need until you're sure you understand exactly what's involved. In this situation, people often do themselves in because they're so anxious about not wanting to appear uninformed. They think that their lack of knowledge in one area of business or finance makes them seem unintelligent in general. Not knowing the facts about something is not the same thing as being unintelligent. In reality, people who ask questions and check into all the details of their business and financial arrangements are not considered stupid. They are thought to be people who are smart enough to investigate details so they can make a well-informed decision.

Communication is a two-way street, an exchange between a speaker and a listener. Your job is to understand; the job of the person talking is to make himself understood. If you ask questions, you may very well find that he hasn't clearly expressed his thought. When the person says it again in another way, you'll see what was meant. And with a little bit more explanation, you'll probably grasp a new or unfamiliar idea.

Don't be afraid of what you don't immediately understand. Consider the example of Andrea, who was an architect just starting out in Toronto. She was required to draw up plans according to specifications written by someone else. When she didn't understand the instructions right away, she assumed: "I'm slow, I'm stupid, they'll find out now that I don't belong in this job." She hated to go back and ask questions, thinking that this would imply she was incompetent.

But Andrea began to practice asking questions. And she found out that, many times, her superior hadn't written the specifications down clearly. *No one* could have understood them. He was simply a bit lazy about writing things out in a complete form. He also seemed to enjoy the social interaction when she had to come ask him about the work. Together, they sorted out what needed to be done.

By asking these questions, Andrea saved herself many hours of anxiety over trying to understand what *couldn't* be understood without further explanation. She also stopped torturing herself over whether the reason she hadn't understood was because she was incompetent.

One other point. When you ask a question, you

often find out that other people didn't understand either, but were afraid to say so. Haven't you ever seen this happen in a meeting or classroom? Someone else raises a question you have in your mind but didn't dare ask. The department head or teacher is happy to oblige with an explanation. Afterwards, you find out that no one else in the room had understood, until that one brave person spoke up. If you don't understand something, the odds are other people don't either.

A particularly important time to keep yourself honest and open is during a performance event—something you're about to do that is significant to you. IP victims tend to make the problem worse by trying to conceal their nervousness. They tell themselves: "If people see that I'm nervous and lack confidence, they'll think it's because I don't know what I'm doing." But the problem is only compounded by their anxiety about exposure and the effort required to appear confident, or just *not* nervous.

Sometimes it's helpful to let others know you feel nervous. You have to decide if your situation is one in which you have some leeway to show this feeling. I would agree that an airline pilot or a surgeon is definitely *not* in a position to tell other people he is nervous as he is about to go to work.

However, if you can express some nervousness in your situation, then you have one less thing to hide. You can use the energy that goes into disguising it to concentrate on what's happening at the moment. It would certainly be acceptable for a student about to take an oral exam to say: "To tell you the truth, I'm feeling a bit nervous. Let me take a minute to compose myself before we get started." Being nervous on a first date is also an acceptable condition that can be admitted; it may even lead to a fascinating conversation. Most people are not sadists. They won't laugh hysterically or tell you you'll never work in this town again.

They will be far more likely to attempt to put you at ease. Then your nervousness is out in the open and you can focus on the matter at hand.

If you're just starting out in a new job, no one would expect you to know everything. Part of what you should be doing right now is asking questions and finding out what your role entails. Seek out "consultants." Talk to someone else who's already familiar with what you're doing and ask about what it requires—other people who've been working at your company for a while, or someone else who's been working for himself. You can probably pick up useful information at the meetings of industry associations.

Set up a support system with people you can rely on and trust. Co-workers can consult and help each other out. Physicians, for example, often consult with one another on difficult cases. Maybe there is someone you can confide in about your deadline anxieties or your nervousness about making that sale. If you're a new parent, talk with other parents and ask the advice of someone who's already been through the early years of child-rearing. If you've been promoted to a new job, talk to others who have held the same position.

One highly capable woman described how she had felt inept and unqualified when she was assigned the planning of a company press conference in New York. A wise friend pointed out to her: "You're not unqualified, you're just inexperienced." There's a big difference.

4. TAKING CONTROL

Sometimes the pressure of concealing those areas in which you feel weak can increase your anxiety to the point where it becomes completely unmanageable. Look for some way in which you can take control of the situation, so you're not just "waiting for the boom to fall." What *exactly* should you know to perform well in your role—or just to relieve your anxiety? Can you pinpoint exactly what you feel is lacking in your knowledge? If so, you may be able to stop worrying about "things in general" and find that there are really only a few specific weaknesses that are troubling you. Chances are there is someplace or someone to provide you with just what you need to know.

Here is how two different people were able to take control of the situations they were afraid would expose them as frauds:

A research analyst from Minnesota told me how she feared that her boss would assign her a project she had never done before. This, she expected, would be her undoing. Her anxiety about this possibility grew so intense, she would feel helpless and paralyzed whenever she contemplated it.

I suggested to her that she make a list of the kinds of tasks with which she was unfamiliar, but might receive as part of a project one day. Once she had it down on paper, she found that this amounted to four or five different things. She gave the list to her boss and asked to be assigned projects that included these tasks, one at a time, when they came up. This way, she could gradually learn what she didn't know. Just by turning over her list to the boss, she lessened her anxiety. She had taken control of the situation, instead of waiting helplessly and letting it control her.

Another woman was a junior executive in Los Angeles who had recently transferred into a different department within her firm. Her new boss expected her to write up reports on the department meetings. This was a task she had never felt confident about doing. Yet she was afraid to tell her boss about this weakness. She felt ashamed when she found he had completely changed her first report. She believed she had been exposed as an incompetent failure.

To gain a sense of control, she finally went to her boss to ask where she could get some training in this area. She was surprised to find out that he didn't think her report had been that bad after all. He told her he actually enjoyed writing and liked to reorganize these reports in his own way. As a matter of fact, he had done the same thing with all her predecessors. She now knew that she hadn't been perceived as incompetent at all. She went on to take a writing course, which improved her confidence even more.

In personal situations, don't worry obsessively about possible scenarios. If, for example, you have fears about having to take care of an aging parent or spouse, make a constructive and realistic plan to prepare for it. Just having a plan will ease your anxiety.

5. PRACTICE BEING YOUR OWN PERSON

If you have difficulty disagreeing with other people and expressing your own views, you have to pay attention to the times when you see this happening.

Little by little, begin to practice saying what you think. If you risk being yourself—gradually, in small ways, step by step—you will find out that most people are capable of accepting expressions of individuality and disagreement. Eventually, you can also begin to accept these aspects of yourself.

Start practicing with someone you like, someone you know cares about you. When you become less anxious about expressing yourself to this person, you can move on to others. Finally, when you have gained more confidence, work on being yourself around the one person who makes you the most anxious.

I know this is easier said than done, but if you can take the risk of speaking up, you are likely to find yourself being rewarded. In the classroom, for example, most teachers won't interpret disagreement with their statements as proof of ignorance. They're usually pleased to find that someone is actually thinking about what they're saying and is interested enough to form an opinion. The students who never contribute anything to the general discussion don't make much of an impression as great intellects. Besides, you have a good chance of making a valid point that will add to everyone's understanding. At the very least, you've expressed yourself and shown that you're an actively thinking human being, not someone content to be spoon-fed information.

Disagreeing with your boss in the office requires more subtlety. Of course, the boss usually makes the final decision about what path to take on a project. Still, he or she will appreciate your contribution if you are able to state a point of view that hasn't yet been considered. An intelligent and efficient boss doesn't have tunnel vision.

The boss needs other people's help. He or she can't operate in a vacuum. As the head of a multimillion-dollar company commented to me, a person in his position "must work with department heads; this can be both good and bad. You can be threatened by them. But you can derive tremendous support from them also."

You might begin by saying something like: "Let me just play devil's advocate here for a minute," and give your point of view. You are showing that you're thoughtful enough to have considered all the ramifications of the problem. Just be sure that the way you disagree with a superior is tactful and doesn't appear to be simply a power struggle. That way, the person is free to consider your point of view without losing face.

If you can present your ideas to the boss in a style that doesn't threaten him, it will certainly be to your credit if your ideas eventually save him from making a mistake. And, here, too, you have a reasonable chance of making a valid point. If you are wrong, you have at least shown that you can think for yourself and have something to contribute.

What if you can't bring yourself to disagree with the people in your personal life? First you have to remind yourself that disagreeing doesn't make you a *disagreeable* person. Once you have expressed your own feelings, you won't have to hide the frustration and resentment that can eat you up inside. And you'll have one less thing to feel fraudulent about.

If you don't like the movie or restaurant your friend or lover has chosen, state your preference. Take turns choosing movies, or compromise on a third restaurant. If you don't agree with that person's opinion of a play, why pretend otherwise? Ask yourself if the relationship is really based on your having to be a carbon copy of that other person. If it is, chances are it's not very gratifying for either of you. Most people like talking to somebody who offers something other than an echo of themselves. You will be a more interesting person when you express what you think and feel.

Good friendships and romantic relationships usually require not only that two people have some things in common, but also that they can tolerate disagreement with one another. The more you express yourself, the less you will have to hide from the other person. This enhances intimacy and cohesiveness between the two of you. It also rids you of underlying anger and resentment that could eventually destroy the relationship.

June was a young woman who had great trouble expressing anger toward her friends. But she finally decided to take the risk. On several occasions, her friend Maxine had made plans to come over and then canceled at the last minute. June called her friend and pointed out what she had been doing. She told Maxine how hurt and angry this lack of consideration made her feel. At first, Maxine began to make excuses; then she simply apologized. She hadn't realized the effect her behavior was having on the friendship.

The issue had been brought into the open before June's anger grew into bitterness. Their friendship continued to flourish and June stopped feeling fraudulent because she had ceased hiding her true feelings.

6. CHANGING YOUR IP HABITS

You can also tackle the Impostor Phenomenon from the angle of your behavior. The IP involves many habits that are persistent and hard to change. You'll have to start small and work your way up.

You may have heard of something called behavioral therapy. In this approach, the situation that is a problem for someone is broken down into a series of steps. Those steps are arranged in order, going from what causes him the least anxiety up to the most. He is helped in overcoming his problem by focusing first on what is least anxiety-provoking and building from there. We've already talked about some of these kinds of "easiest-to-hardest" techniques.

The various IP behavior patterns and habits can be approached in the same way. Do you relate to the behavior of an IP Workaholic? A Shrinking Violet? A Chameleon? Observe your own behavior and learn when you are showing signs of the IP in your actions. Then work on changing that behavior. Here are some of the ways in which you can do this.

A. *Teach Yourself to Accept Compliments*

The Shrinking Violet's pattern is to immediately reject, devalue, disown, or suspect any compliments he or she receives. Sometimes, through sheer will-power, you can teach yourself to curb this kind of automatic reaction to praise.

Whenever you get a compliment, words of praise, or some form of admiration from someone else, say, "Thank you," and stop right there. If you are used to responding to compliments with an "Oh, no, it was nothing," this may be a real struggle for you. At first, *literally* limit your response to the two words "Thank you." Smile. But don't say another word about the subject at hand. You must avoid the urge to make those comments about how it really wasn't such a good job, you could have improved this part of it if you'd had more time, and so on.

After you're comfortable with that first step, you might want to add something to the "Thank you" that shows more of your appreciation to the person who offered the praise. Compliment him or her in return. For example: "Thank you, it's kind of you to say so . . . it's nice of you to notice . . . that means a lot to me, coming from you." All of these phrases focus on the *other* person, not you or your performance. Stay away from those areas lest you wander back into dangerous territory and find yourself making excuses for your accomplishment.

When you do resist the temptation to devalue a compliment, give yourself a reward. It could be anything you enjoy—a chocolate bar, a relaxing swim, a nice dinner.

Maybe you have already learned to restrain yourself and act graciously when you receive recognition or praise. You can accept the compliment externally. But what about internally?

Try to absorb the compliment and let it make you feel good. Think about it again and again during the day. Allow it to nourish your self-image.

Just after you get a compliment, once you're by yourself again, try writing it down. We sometimes get praise that comes along with a minor piece of criticism ("You gave a wonderful talk at the meeting yesterday. Too bad the client looked so sour when you told that joke."). Some people find they later remember the critical part without any problem—but what was that nice thing the person said? Gone, or only fuzzy in their memories. So get it down on paper right away.

Accept a compliment for what it is: someone letting you know that you have done something good, you have been successful. Let it end there. Don't pursue the negative thoughts that might erupt. Catch yourself if you start musing: "Now, I'll have too much to live up to next time," or "I wonder what she wants from me," or "What a fool he must be! He didn't even realize that I forgot to cite the two most obvious precedents." Stop those thoughts! Compliments should give you some added reassurance. They should help dispel self-doubts, not add to them. Replace the negative thoughts with positive ones.

The person who has praised you has noticed the general effect of what you've done. The general effect is what counts, not the insignificant details. He doesn't care about minor flaws. Yes, minor flaws do count if you're launching spaceships. But if small errors in your work are that critical, you wouldn't have gotten a compliment in the first place if you'd made any mistakes that had significance. If you receive a compliment, someone thought enough of you to offer it. That's what you have to remember.

B. *Experiment with Your Work Patterns*

If you have the habits of an IP Workaholic, you should take a long, hard look at how you approach new projects. Force yourself to arrange your priorities and to spend less time on those tasks that are the least important. Vary your behavior. You will have to take some small risks in order to find out that every task doesn't demand the same amount of your time and effort.

Experiment. If you are in the habit of laboriously revising your letters, write a letter just once, and resist the urge to go over it again and again until it's perfect. If you take copious notes at every meeting, decide that at the next general discussion or brainstorming session, you will listen carefully, but only make a summarizing note every two or three minutes. Have a spontaneous get-together for a few friends, instead of planning an elaborate dinner party. If you are a woman suffering from IP feelings about your appearance, and devote hours to getting dressed each day, very gradually decrease the amount of makeup you put on before doing errands in the neighborhood. Again, start small and work your way up to the things that are most difficult for you.

C. *Break the Worry Ritual*

Do you have the IP Magical Thinker's habit of always envisioning failure? You must allow yourself to envision success instead. Make a contract with yourself: For one week, you will balance every pessimistic thought of failure with an optimistic one about success. In the second week, allow yourself only one or two pessimistic thoughts per day. Once you've used up your allotment for the day, tell yourself that the next negative thought will have to wait for tomorrow—you've got the rest of today "off."

As you change the habit of superstitious thinking, you will learn that you can succeed without the same degree of advance worrying. Gradually, you'll find that you can rely less and less on the worry ritual.

7. REVISING YOUR EGO IDEAL

In Chapter 3, I talked about the ego ideal, the internal standard by which we measure ourselves. IP victims often have an unrealistic image of what the self *should* be. No matter what they've done, they tend to feel it isn't *good* enough. Their ego ideal is a perfectionistic one.

You may need to revise your ego ideal so that it comes closer to being realistic. Does your sense of what you should be or should be able to achieve lean toward perfection? The idea that it's shameful not to be perfect is a surefire way to convince yourself that you're a failure, despite what the world thinks of your accomplishments.

In order to change your ego ideal for yourself, you first have to discover what it really is. This is one of the times family "labels" and "myths" come into the picture. Think back to when you were between the ages of six and twelve. What did you feel your family expected of you? How did they describe you? What were the family stories told about you—the kind of child you were, and the things you were good (or bad) at? Did you feel you should always gets straight A's, come up with something brilliant to say, or win every competition you entered? Maybe you were told you were always sweet and generous, kept everybody entertained, or were the best-liked one in your family and your class at school. Perhaps your relatives had very high expectations of what you would do when you grew up.

This may be where you got your original ideas about the standard to which you should adhere. How much did you feel that love and acceptance depended on your playing your role to perfection? If you couldn't always be perfect, did you hide your "failures" from the family? Think about how this pattern continued through your adolescence and into your adult life.

To revise an ego ideal that demands perfection, the next step is to redefine the word "failure." When is a mistake "failure" and when is it *just a mistake?* The Impostor Phenomenon can lead you to that "all or none" thinking, in which success equals perfection and anything less than perfection equals failure.

I recently heard a story about a young boy in high school. He was considered a genius and had always received straight A's in school. The day he got his first B, he hanged himself. This is an extreme and tragic example of how people can feel like failures without reason and how mercilessly they punish themselves for it.

If you have to give a speech or presentation, do you agonize about failing if you mispronounce a word, stammer, or stumble? What if an error slipped by in a report you've written? Do you believe you've lost or failed if you come in second in a competition? Maybe you've been working late all week and you suddenly discover your children have been eating cookies and ice cream for dinner five nights straight. Are you a failure as a parent? Or your fiancé calls off the wedding and leaves for Tahiti with his old girlfriend. Does that mean you chose the wrong person, or neglected him?

All of these situations can seem like very real and devastating failures to someone who expects himself to be perfect. Many IP victims look at such incidents from their past and torment themselves with the "proof" that they are failures. They believe that these things must be hidden from others to maintain their images as successful in their roles.

A mistake is a human error, not a fatal flaw that must be camouflaged forever. Sometimes, certain factors are just beyond our control. If you feel you must hide your mistakes out of shame, then you are trying to appear perfect—better than anyone else. Of course, you should try to do the best you're capable of in your career and in your personal life. You shouldn't stop striving to achieve, or settle for something less than you desire. But having to be number one and perfect *all the time in everything* is a very grandiose aim. You are setting yourself up for disappointment.

Ask yourself how you would respond if a friend told you that he or she had made the same mistake you made. Would you feel your friend was a failure? Would you even care very much about the mistake? How long would it take before you forgot about it? Chances are, it would have little effect on your overall opinion of your friend. You might even like him better for being vulnerable. Treat yourself as reasonably as you would your friend.

Next, try telling someone you like and trust about one or two mistakes you made in the past. It could be anything from a social gaffe that left you mortified to a major business mistake. Perhaps you can tell this person that you feel the mistake meant you were a failure. Once you've brought this feeling out into the open, the power of its secrecy will be lost. All the energy you've put into concealing it will be freed for more productive and enjoyable things. You'll probably feel closer to the other person, because you've shared a secret. In fact, he may like you *better* for simply being human, not the image of perfection.

There's something to be said for going through the

experience of actually failing at something. I'm not going to suggest that you deliberately fail. But some IP victims have accidentally found that a genuine failure was the best thing that ever happened to them in relieving the anxiety tied to IP feelings.

An accountant I know with IP feelings failed her CPA exam. Yet life went on the same as before. No one who knew her thought she was stupid. She didn't lose her job. Her clients didn't disappear. The "worst" that happened was that she had to study and take it over again. Life doesn't come to a screeching halt for the person who fails a certification exam, the athlete who doesn't win a big event, or the executive who doesn't get promoted one year.

Think about what would constitute a major failure for you. Then make a list of the consequences you fear would follow this failure if everyone knew about it. Write down your true gut feelings. Would you lose your job or all your friends? Be disowned by your family? Become a social pariah? Never work again? Be forced to sleep in the street? Be put in jail? Write down every possibility that you secretly fear.

When you're finished, go back over your list and ask yourself how likely it is that each of these things would actually happen. Is it 100 percent likely? 75 percent? 40 percent? 10 percent? Zero? When you see that the things you're afraid of really aren't likely to take place, force yourself to remember that percent figure the next time you're panicked about the possibility of failing.

By examining whether your fears of a failure's consequences are real, you are employing a specific psychological approach. You're using your intellect to test what might be irrational or illogical ideas and assumptions. Two forms of psychotherapy are based on this approach: cognitive techniques and rational-emotive techniques. Your cognitive or rational side—your thinking—can influence what you feel. The idea here is that if we can change our irrational and self-defeating thoughts, we can influence our emotional states.

Cognitive therapy was developed by Dr. Aaron Beck, rational-emotive therapy by Dr. Albert Ellis. In his book *A Guide to Rational Living* (written with Dr. Robert Harper), Ellis described how he used this approach to help a man suffering from the Impostor Phenomenon, well before the syndrome got its name.[1]

This man was a young physicist who had gone to a psychotherapist for help. He seemed to have everything: an excellent reputation in his field, athletic ability, even good looks. Yet, he complained, he was ". . . really a phony. I am living under false pretenses. And the longer it goes on, the more people praise me and make a fuss over my accomplishments, the worse I feel."

The therapist pointed out that experts in the field had examined this man's work and said his ideas were of revolutionary importance. But the physicist presented a list of reasons he felt he was still a phony: He wasted time sitting in his office and staring into space; he didn't always think about problems with clarity and precision; once he had caught himself making a naive mistake; in writing a paper he was taking too many hours, instead of the one or two that should have been necessary. He went on to contrast himself unfavorably with the famous physicist J. Robert Oppenheimer.

The therapist was able to show this young man how unreasonable it was to be so perfectionistic. He noted that many studies of the creative process show that it is an uneven one. No one can be creative all the time. Staring out the window could very well be a necessary step in the mental process of creativity. Eventually, this physicist was able to see that he was striving for perfect achievement. He was able to modify his standards and begin enjoying his work. Without his perfectionism, he became even more productive.

By changing his thoughts, he had changed his feelings.

There are other areas in which this technique can help you prove to yourself that your feelings of fraudulence aren't based on a logical reality. Think about your past successes. Consider how likely it is that someone could really have achieved what you have if he were truly incompetent. How realistic is it to think that anyone who actually was untalented or incapable could have walked into your job or your life and done what you have done?

Look at all the things you can do and are good at. To you, they seem unimportant, worthless—they come easily to you, so they can't mean much. You're wrong. No matter what it is you are good at, there's someone else who can't do that same thing and wishes he or she had that ability. Being good with people, for example, is a highly valued skill. But IP victims often say this is just how they "get by" and shrug it off as nothing, or as a form of manipulation. It doesn't have to mean you manipulate people. It can mean you are able to make people feel comfortable and offer them a positive experience in dealing with you. Another example: IP victims frequently point out that they are articulate, but devalue this as "glibness." Whatever your particular skill is, give yourself credit for it. There are plenty of people who long to have that talent. The same applies to abilities in writing, math, or any other intellectual area.

Have you ever looked at someone else's job or life, and thought, "I could never do what they do"? *They* can manage it, but you're positive you couldn't survive if you had to sell, write, select stocks, or raise three children and hold a job at the same time. Well, somebody's very probably thinking the same thing about what you do. Accept the idea that you have abilities and talents of your own. Write them down and think about how you've used them in the past without giving yourself any credit for them. Acknowledge them as being real.

Use this type of logical thinking to question your beliefs about what constitutes the "true measure" of success or intelligence. Focus on the area you find difficult, and which you believe you should be better at in order to be truly smart or successful. If you think mathematical ability is the measure of intelligence, why do you think this? Do studies of intellectual achievement support that view? What studies? Do experts on intelligence believe that only one aptitude equals intelligence?

If you are concerned with your business acumen, ask yourself the following question: If experts or studies have proved that there is just one skill necessary for having a successful business career, what would that skill be? Is it communication skills, the ability to manage other people, financial savvy? When you reason it through, you will realize that there is no one answer to these questions, no right or wrong.

Maybe you doubt your "skills" as a friend. What does it mean to be a good friend? Does it mean you never get angry, never disagree, always do favors no matter how inconvenient they are? If this is true, why haven't you cut off your friendships in which the other person doesn't do all this for you? For any personal role you play, examine what you expect of yourself. Are you looking for perfection?

Take this approach also to examine situations that might cause the IP to surface. Look around you and observe carefully before you draw conclusions. Do you feel like a fake simply because you feel different in some way from your peers? Is it that you're really incompetent in your role, or simply that you feel you don't belong where you are? Are you the only black, Hispanic, woman, or man in your environment? Do you feel like your success in your role is a "mistake" because you think you're incompetent—or is it just that you would like a different career better?

Test all the ideas about uniqueness that we've already talked about. Do you come from a different social background than most of your peers? Have you surpassed the achievements of others in your family? Carefully examine how you are "different" or unique, and ask yourself whether this might be the cause of your feelings.

Whenever you sense "impostor" feelings coming on, put them through the "reality test." See if they're based on something real, or on an incorrect image of reality caused by your secret fears.

8. "OWNING" YOUR INNER AND OUTER SELVES

To relieve your feeling of being a fake, another idea that you should be thinking about is that of the true and false selves. Do you imagine yourself as having a true inner self (the person you "really" are) and a false outer self (the person you "pretend" to be—the one you think is fooling others)?

In order to see yourself as one, whole, integrated person, you need to resolve the feeling of discrepancy between your public and private self-images. This conflict is especially apparent in IP Genies. Genies adapt their personalities to fit the situation. They give comfort when it is required, they provoke, they challenge, they amuse—whatever it takes to make the other person happy and receptive to them.

What IP victims need to understand is that they are not manipulative, but flexible and multifaceted. They must learn to "own" all the parts of their personalities.

Psychologists have worked with IP victims in the past on "role-playing." In this context, I don't mean playing your role in real life, but pretending and acting out a role or a particular conversation. When you create an imaginary dialogue between yourself and someone else, clues to your true feelings can be found in the "lines" you speak. After all, you're the one determining how this scene plays. Emotions and fears come out spontaneously; you're not trying to analyze yourself or explain away feelings.

With the help of your imagination, you can make some discoveries about the different sides of yourself. Allow yourself to "daydream" and play different parts. If you feel you are too compliant, imagine yourself as assertive and direct. If you doubt your intelligence, play out the idea of being smart. Pay attention to what happens in these imaginary scenes.

This approach is best done with the help of a trained psychotherapist. He or she can guide you in the most constructive direction and aid you in understanding what your "lines" express about your feelings.

Working in therapy, you may discover parts of yourself you didn't even know existed. The overly modest or shy person may discover a fantasy of being the center of attention. The "intellectual" may find he wants to express an artistic drive he never knew he had. This is also an opportunity to learn more about your fears. If you act out the role of being a successful person, you might see that it frightens you in some way. Or you can suddenly come upon feelings of competitiveness, envy, or guilt. Those feelings might have been so intense, you "disowned" them.

By getting in touch with all the different sides of yourself, you can learn that one side of you doesn't make another side invalid. A loving parent, child, or spouse can also be angry and resentful at times. A creative or highly intelligent person may have to struggle in certain areas.

One role-playing exercise some psychologists have used is to ask an IP victim to make a "confession."[2] Think about all the people you have "fooled." In your mind, tell them exactly how you fooled them and imagine how they would react to this confession. The idea is to discover you haven't really "fooled" them. It is only your fear or fantasy that you have.

9. TALKING TO OTHER PEOPLE WHO FEEL AS YOU DO

The secret nature of the Impostor Phenomenon causes its victims to feel alone and isolated with their hidden feelings of phoniness. Being able to give the feelings a name and understanding what they're all about can ease that sense of isolation. But it is even more beneficial to meet and talk with other IP victims.

In a group setting, you can learn that you all share the same fears and experiences, and give one another support. You can also encourage each other to see whether "impostor" feelings might be based on some reality or if they stem only from self-doubts. A group can give you some immediate feedback on how well you're doing in your role at work or at home. And that can lead to your developing your own self-approval.

Unfortunately, there have been far too few IP groups. If you are interested in finding or starting an IP group in your area, you'll have to do some research on the possibilities. But, remember, an IP group should be run *only by a qualified professional*. That means a licensed psychologist or psychiatrist, or a trained therapist working under their supervision. *Do not* attempt to run one on your own or attend a group run by someone who isn't qualified to do so. That could result in great psychological harm to you and to others.

If you would like to pursue the idea of an IP group, ask your family physician if he can recommend a qualified professional with whom you can discuss this idea. You can also call the psychiatry department of the local teaching hospital or your local mental health association. They should be able to give you the names of a few doctors who can help, or at least advise you on what your next step should be. If you're a student, you might talk to someone in the school's student health service or counseling center about it, or to the school psychologist.

I wouldn't suggest that anyone who is already working with a psychotherapist stop their treatment in favor of a group on the Impostor Phenomenon. If you are already in therapy or analysis, discuss the idea of a group with your doctor and see if he feels it might be helpful to you as an individual.

I hope that as we all begin to understand how common this syndrome is, more trained professionals will begin to offer this kind of help for those suffering from the IP.

10. THE OPTION OF PSYCHOTHERAPY

As I noted, all of these suggestions for combating the IP are based on established theories of psychology. For that reason, you may find that you can do even better with them if you work with a qualified psychologist or psychiatrist. Follow the steps I've outlined here on your own, but think about whether it makes sense for you to get some professional help.

If your "impostor" feelings are making you so anxious or depressed that you can't function, or if you feel suicidal, you should seek professional help immediately. And don't write off severe feelings of alienation or difficulties in coping as "just part of the IP, a problem that lots of people have." They may be the result of completely different problems.

There are a few points to consider here. Your feelings of fraudulence might be too strong to be overcome without help. And some of these feelings may be based on experiences or emotions that are buried too deeply in your mind for you to be able to reach them alone. A trained psychiatrist or psychologist can work with you to find out what they are. If you think you are going through a temporary case of the IP, you might be able to get past it more quickly and with less emotional pain if you get some short-term help.

Psychoanalysis or certain kinds of psychotherapy can lead you back to the source of your deepest feelings. By unlocking memories and emotions from the unconscious mind, these approaches can aid you in discovering the motives and fears that have led you to the Impostor Phenomenon.

Here are some of the steps you can follow to find a qualified therapist:

Ask your family doctor, or any other medical doctor who is treating you, to recommend a psychiatrist or licensed clinical psychologist.

Call the best hospital in your area or a teaching hospital, and ask for a few referrals from their department of psychiatry.

Ask for a referral from your local mental health association or local society of clinical psychologists.

Consult the National Register of Health Service Providers in Psychology to find the name of a psychologist who has met their required standards.

If you can't afford private psychotherapy, go to the outpatient department of psychiatry at a teaching hospital. There you may work with a resident in psychiatry or a postdoctoral psychologist who is being supervised by more senior professionals. You can also go to your local community mental health center.

When you find a qualified therapist you like and feel comfortable with (or if you are already seeing one), ask if he is familiar with the Impostor Phenomenon. If not, show him this book.

11. HELPING OTHERS

Perhaps you suspect that someone you care about is suffering from the Impostor Phenomenon. If you would like to help that person, there are a few things you might do.

You can probably recognize signs of the IP in his behavior. You know what the outward signs are. When you offer him a compliment, he instantly points out what was wrong with what he did. Or you hear him starting to express an opinion about something and notice that he changes in midstream once he realizes your opinion differs. After a success, he drops remarks like "Oh, that was just good luck" or "They couldn't find anybody else for the job."

Be sensitive to those times when he's experiencing "impostor" feelings and take his feelings seriously. Maybe you've heard him say a hundred times he's definitely going to blow it *this* time—but he never does. Don't tell him that he's being ridiculous and anyone can see how terrific he is. Understand that this feeling is just as real and frightening to him each time he experiences it.

Let him know that you like him for who he is and not for some public image he thinks he has. Help him to realize that you appreciate that he has more than only one dimension as a person. In a tactful and supportive way, point out when he is showing the signs of IP behavior.

Be sympathetic and try to create a climate in which he feels he can talk about the problem. Just getting rid of the secrecy can be an enormous burden off his shoulders. If he is extremely anxious or depressed, discuss the possibility of his talking with a good therapist.

And give him this book to read.

"The terrible secret" is now out in the open. So remember, you aren't alone. The feeling of being an impostor, fake, or fraud can simply be the Impostor Phenomenon at work. If you let it, it can hold you back from accomplishing all you should in life. And it will steal from you the pleasure and satisfaction that should come from your success. Hold on tight to those good feelings. You earned them.

Notes

CHAPTER 1: THE TERRIBLE SECRET

1. Joan C. Harvey, "The Impostor Phenomenon and Achievement: A Failure to Internalize Success" (doctoral dissertation, Temple University, 1981). *Dissertation Abstracts International*, 1982, *42*, 4969B-4970B. Ann Arbor, MI: University Microfilms No. 8210500.

2. Pauline Rose Clance and Suzanne Ament Imes, "The Impostor Phenomenon in High Achieving Women: Dynamics and Therapeutic Intervention," *Psychotherapy: Theory, Research and Practice*, Vol. 15, No. 3, Fall, 1978.

3. Jeanne M. Stahl, Henrie M. Turner, Alfreedia E. Wheeler, and Phyllis B. Elbert, "The 'Impostor Phenomenon' in High School and College Science Majors." Paper presented at the meeting of the American Psychological Association, Montreal, 1980, pp. 3–4.

4. Margaret S. Gibbs, Ph.D., Karen Alter-Reid, and Sharon DeVries, "Instrumentality and the Impostor Phenomenon." Paper presented at the meeting of the American Psychological Association, Toronto, 1984.

5. Gail M. Matthews, "Impostor Phenomenon: Attributions for Success and Failure." Paper presented at the meeting of the American Psychological Association, Toronto, 1984.

6. Mary E. H. Topping, "The Impostor Phenomenon: A Study of Its Construct and Incidence in University Faculty Members" (doctoral dissertation, University of South Florida, 1983). *Dissertation Abstracts International, 44*, 1948–

1949B. Ann Arbor, MI: University Microfilms No. 8316534.

7. Stahl et al., op cit.

8. Gail Matthews and Pauline Clance also talked about the IP victim's feelings about "what counts" in their presentation "Treatment of the Impostor Phenomenon in Psychotherapy Clients" at the Midwinter Convention of Divisions 29 and 42 of the American Psychological Association, San Diego, 1984.

9. Topping, op. cit.

10. Matthews, op. cit.

CHAPTER 2: HIDING THE SECRET

1. Clance and Imes, op. cit., p. 244.

2. Stahl et al., op. cit., p. 4.

3. H. H. Kelley, *Causal Schemata and the Attribution Process*. Monograph. Morristown, NJ: General Learning Press, 1972.

4. David Shapiro, *Autonomy and Rigid Character*. New York, NY: Basic Books, 1981.

5. Clance and Imes, op. cit., pp. 244–245.

CHAPTER 3: FEELING LIKE A FAKE IN YOUR PERSONAL LIFE

1. Philip G. Zimbardo, *Shyness*. Reading, MA: Addison-Wesley Publishing Company, 1977.

2. Sigmund Freud, "On Narcissism: An Introduction," in *A General Selection From the Works of Sigmund Freud*, ed. John Rickman. New York, NY: Doubleday/Anchor Books, 1957.

3. Leon Festinger, *A Theory of Cognitive Dissonance*. Evanston, IL: Row Peterson, 1957.

4. William James, "The Consciousness of Self," in *The Principles of Psychology*, 2 vols. New York, NY: Henry Holt, 1890; reprint ed. Dover Publications, 1950.

5. Erving Goffman, *The Presentation of Self in Everyday Life*. (Edinburgh: University of Edinburgh Social Sciences Research Center, 1958; reprinted by Doubleday, 1959).

6. Kenneth J. Gergen, "The Social Construction of Self-Knowledge," in T. Mischel, ed., *The Self: Psychological*

and Philosophical Issues. Totowa, NJ: Rowman and Little-field, 1977.

7. Mark Snyder has written extensively about the self-monitor. The specifics I talk about here come from the following sources:

Social Psychology by Lawrence S. Wrightsman in collaboration with others. Monterey, CA: Brooks/Cole Publishing Company, division of Wadsworth Publishing Company, Inc., second edition, 1977. Chapter titled "Impression Management" by Mark Snyder.

Mark Snyder, "Self-Monitoring Processes," *Advances in Experimental Social Psychology*, Vol. 12, 1979.

Psychological Perspectives on the Self, J. Suls, ed., Hillsdale, NJ: Laurence Erlbaum Associates, 1982. Chapter titled "Self-Monitoring: The Self in Action" by Mark Snyder and Bruce H. Campbell.

Mark Snyder, "The Many Me's of the Self-Monitor," *Psychology Today*, March 1980.

Mark Snyder, "Self-Monitoring of Expressive Behavior," *Journal of Personality and Social Psychology*, Vol. 30, No. 4, 1974. *Psychology Today*, March, 1980, p. 92.

8. Edward E. Sampson, "Personality and the Location of Identity," *Journal of Personality*, 1978, pp. 552–568.

9. D. L. Rarick, G. F. Soldow, and R. S. Geizer, "Self-Monitoring as a Mediator of Conformity," *Central States Speech Journal*, 1976, 27(4), pp. 267–271.

10. "The Legacy of Peter Sellers," editorial, *The Philadelphia Inquirer* (Friday, July 25, 1980).

11. Desmond Ryan, "Peter Sellers: A Requiem for a Comedy Genius," *The Philadelphia Inquirer* (Sunday, July 27, 1980).

12. Donald W. Winnicott, "Ego Distortion in Terms of the True and False Self," in D. W. Winnicott, ed., *The Maturational Process and the Facilitating Environment*. (New York, NY: International Universities Press, 1965).

13. Norma K. Lawler, "Impostor Phenomenon: Two Treatment Approaches." Paper presented at the meeting of the American Psychological Association, Toronto, August 1984.

CHAPTER 4: DO YOU BELIEVE YOU'RE AN IMPOSTOR?

1. Kelley, op. cit.

CHAPTER 5: HOW IT HAPPENS—IN THE FAMILY

1. Suzanne Imes and Pauline Clance have written about their approach in adapting Adlerian life-style questionnaires to discern "early script messages and decisions" in "Treatment of the Impostor Phenomenon in High-Achieving Women," *Women Therapists Working With Women*, Claire M. Brody, ed., New York, NY: Springer Publishing Company, 1984, pp. 75–78. I have also found this approach to be a useful one.

2. Pauline Rose Clance and Suzanne Ament Imes, "The Impostor Phenomenon in High Achieving Women: Dynamics and Therapeutic Intervention," op. cit., p. 243.

3. Ibid. Clance and Imes described this as a second typical IP pattern.

4. Sigmund Freud, *Inhibitions, Symptoms, and Anxiety* (1926), in James Strachey, ed., Standard Edition of *The Complete Psychological Works of Sigmund Freud, 20,* London, England: Hogarth Press, 1955–1974, pp. 77–175.

5. Sigmund Freud, "Those Wrecked by Success," in "Some Character Types Met With in Psychoanalytical Work," *Collected Papers*. New York, NY: Basic Books, 1959.

6. David W. Krueger, *Success and the Fear of Success in Women*. New York, NY: The Free Press, 1984.

CHAPTER 6: HOW IT HAPPENS—IN THE WORLD AROUND YOU

1. Michael Penland and Susan McCammon, "The Impostor Phenomenon: Feelings of Intellectual Phoniness in Higher Achievers." Paper presented at The Second Teaching/Learning About Women Conference, Roanoke College, April 1984.

2. Pauline Clance, "The Dynamics and Treatment of the Impostor Phenomenon in High-Achieving Persons," South-

eastern Psychological Association Presidential Address, Atlanta, Georgia, March 1983.

3. Pauline Rose Clance and Suzanne Ament Imes, "The Impostor Phenomenon in High Achieving Women: Dynamics and Therapeutic Intervention," op. cit.

4. Kay Deaux, "Sex and the Attribution Process," in J. H. Harvey, W. J. Ickes, and R. F. Kidd, eds., *New Directions in Attribution Research*, Vol. 1. New York, NY: Halsted Press, 1976, pp. 335–352.

5. J. Bardwick, E. Douvan, M. Horner, and D. Guttman, eds., *Feminine Personality and Conflict*. Belmont, CA: Brooks/Cole Publishing Company, division of Wadsworth Publishing Company, Inc., 1970. Chapter titled "Femininity and Successful Achievement—A Basic Inconsistency" by Martina S. Horner.

6. Lynn Monahan, Deanna Kuhn, and Phillip Shaver, "Intrapsychic Versus Cultural Explanations of the 'Fear of Success' Motive," *Journal of Personality and Social Psychology*, 1974, 29(1), 60–64.

7. Madeline Hirschfeld, "The Impostor Phenomenon in Successful Career Women." Paper presented at the meeting of the American Psychological Association, Washington, D.C., 1982.

8. Stahl et al., op. cit.

9. Suzanne Imes, "The Impostor Phenomenon as a Function of Attribution Patterns and Internalized Femininity/Masculinity in High Achieving Women and Men" (doctoral dissertation, Georgia State University, 1979). *Dissertation Abstracts International*, 1980, *40*, 5868B–5869B. Ann Arbor, MI: University Microfilm No. 8013056.

10. Joan C. Harvey, "Impostor Phenomenon Among High Achievers: The Experience of True and False Selves," Special Topics Paper, Department of Psychology, Temple University, 1980.

11. The Harvey Impostor Phenomenon (IP) Scale was developed as a substantially reliable and valid, self-administered, time-efficient method for measuring the Impostor Phenomenon. Following the rational-empirical approach for test construction, an initial pool of 21 items were written in the form of declarative statements, to which individuals

could respond on a 7-point scale, ranging from "Not at all true" to "Very true" about themselves. The items were then empirically tested with a sample of 74 male and female graduate students. The initial items were theoretically based on and derived from three sources: the interview data of Clance and Imes (1978); the survey data collected by Stahl et al. (1980); and my own observations of the body of literature from psychology, sociology, and psychoanalysis related to the "false self" concept (Harvey, 1980).

Following a statistical analysis of the data collected on each item and on total scale scores, I retained the items that were most internally consistent with each other, and the most reliable predictors of a total Impostor Phenomenon Score. Fourteen of the original 21 items—the ones proved to be the most reliable—were retained. This final 14-item scale was then cross-validated in a second sample of 72 under-graduate students. It proved to be substantially reliable. In a later replication by Dr. Mary Topping (1983) in a sample of 285 university faculty members, the 14-item Harvey IP Scale again showed a similar degree of reliability.

I also collected evidence to establish a degree of validity for the scale. I found that high Impostor Phenomenon scores were significantly related to having a history of high achievement; i.e., high scores were more prevalent in a sample of honors students than in a sample of more typical students. And high scores were also more prevalent in honors students who attributed a portion of their success to their interpersonal assets than in those who did not. Topping (1983) found a substantial correlation between high scores on the Harvey IP Scale and high levels of trait anxiety as measured by the instrument developed by Charles Spielberger.

To further validate the IP Scale, I collected evidence that showed it was statistically different from instruments that measure constructs that sound similar in nature; specifically, self-monitoring as measured by Mark Snyder's self-monitoring scale, and low self-esteem as measured by Rosenberg's self-esteem scale.

12. Joan C. Harvey, Louise H. Kidder, and Lynn Sutherland, "The Impostor Phenomenon and Achievement: Issues of Sex, Race, and Self-Perceived Atypicality." Paper pre-

sented at the meeting of the American Psychological Association, Los Angeles, 1981. Ann Arbor, MI: ERIC Document Reproduction Service No. ED212966.

13. Frances Cherry and Kay Deaux, "Fear of Success Versus Fear of Gender-Inconsistent Behavior: A Sex Similarity." Paper presented at the meeting of the Midwestern Psychological Association, Chicago, May 1975.

14. Linda Loyd, "Penn State Tries to Be More Inviting to Blacks," *The Philadelphia Inquirer,* February 10, 1985.

15. William J. McGuire, Claire V. McGuire, Pamela Child, and Terry Fujioka, "Salience of Ethnicity in the Spontaneous Self-Concept as a Function of One's Ethnic Distinctiveness in the Social Environment," *Journal of Personality and Social Psychology,* 1978, *36,* pp. 511–520.

16. Paul R. Abramson, Philip A. Goldberg, Judith H. Greenberg, and Linda Abramson, "The Talking Platypus Phenomenon: Competency Ratings as a Function of Sex and Professional Status," *Psychology of Women Quarterly,* 1977, *2*(2), pp. 114–124.

17. Reported by Jeff Meer, "Special Stress for Black Professors," *Psychology Today,* October 1984, p. 11.

CHAPTER 7: THROWING AWAY THE MASK

1. Albert Ellis and Robert A. Harper, *A Guide to Rational Living.* No. Hollywood, CA: Wilshire Book Company, 1971, p. 99.

2. Imes and Clance wrote about this particular gestalt exercise in "Treatment of the Impostor Phenomenon in High-Achieving Women," *Women Therapists Working With Women,* op. cit., pp. 78–79.

The Finest Books For

TODAY'S WOMAN IN TODAY'S WORLD

Men and women, the young and the old, first-generation professionals, people in new and unfamiliar roles— anyone can suffer from the IMPOSTOR PHENOMENON!

- Paige, the "workaholic," attributes her success to Herculean efforts and constant overwork, and *not* to her ability.
- Kerry, the "magical thinker," believes her coercive, ritualistic worrying ensures positive results.
- John, the "shrinking violet," can't accept praise. He feels any display of pride will be punished by a humiliating failure.
- Lucy, the "charmer," thinks her personality and social skills outweigh her *true* abilities and talents.

Do you recognize yourself, or anyone you know? Remember, you are not alone. You *can* break free of the Impostor Phenomenon. Your success, your talents, your achievements belong to *you*. Start owning them right now!

_____

"Timely and well-written . . . shows how to start appreciating your own talents and stop being afraid of success."

—*Publishers Weekly*

_____

"It's amazing how many people in the public eye, including athletes, feel like they are merely lucky or are going to be found out, no matter how great their success. Many never accept their own talents. This unusual book deals with the subject in a helpful way."

—Don Meredith

_____

"A superb book on a very important subject . . ."

—George Weinberg, Ph.D., psychologist and author of *The Heart of Psychotherapy* and *Self Creation*